SHEPHERD'S NOTES
Christian Classics

GW00384127

SHEPHERD'S NOTES
Christian Classics

Calvin's
Institutes of the
Christian Religion

HOLMAN
REFERENCE

NASHVILLE, TENNESSEE

Shepherd's Notes—John Calvin's *Institutes of the Christian Religion*
© 1998
by B&H Publishing Group
Nashville, Tennessee
All rights reserved
Printed in the United States of America

978-0-8054-9200-2
Dewey Decimal Classification: 230.42
Subject Heading: CALVIN
Library of Congress Card Catalog Number: 98–21466

The quotations from Calvin's *Institutes of the Christian Religion* are from the translation by John McNeil from the Library of Christian Classic Series. Used by permission of The Westminister/John Knox Press.

Unless otherwise stated all Scripture citation is from the HOLY BIBLE, NEW INTERNATIONAL VERSION®. Copyright © 1973, 1978, 1984 by International Bible Society. Used by permission of Zondervan Publishing House. All Rights Reserved. The "NIV" and "New International Version" trademarks are registered in the United States Patent and Trademark Office by International Bible Society. Use of either trademark requires the permission of International Bible Society.

Library of Congress Cataloging-in-Publication Data

DeVries,Mark.
John Calvin's Institutes of the Christian religion / Mark DeVries, editor [i.e. author] ; Kirk Freeman, general editor.
     p. cm. — (Shepherd's notes. Christian classics)
    Includes bibliographical references.
    ISBN 0–8054–9200–3
    1. Calvin, Jean, 1509–1564. Institutio Christianae religionis. 2. Reformed Church—Doctrines. 3. Theology, Doctrinal. I. Kirk Freeman, 1966–
II. Title. III. Series.
  BX9420.I69D48   1998
  230'.42—dc21

                                       98–21466
                                         CIP

2 3 4 5 6   14 13 12 11

CONTENTS

Foreword vi

How to Use This Book vii

Introduction 1

Prefatory Address to King Francis 12

Book One: The Knowledge of God

    the Creator 15

Book Two: The Knowledge of God the

    Redeemer in Christ 27

Book Three: The Means, the Benefits,

    and the Effects of Grace 57

Bibliography 85

Dear Reader:

Shepherd's Notes—Classics Series is designed to give you a quick, step-by-step overview of some of the enduring treasures of the Christian faith. They are designed to be used alongside the classic itself—either in individual study or in a study group.

Classics have staying power. Although they were written in a particular place and time and often in response to situations different than our own, they deal with problems, concerns, and themes that transcend time and place.

The faithful of all generations have found spiritual nourishment in the Scriptures and in the works of Christians from earlier generations. Martin Luther and John Calvin would not have become who they were apart from their reading Augustine. God used the writings of Martin Luther to move John Wesley from a religion of dead works to an experience at Aldersgate in which his "heart was strangely warmed."

It is an awesome sight—these streams of gracious influence flowing from generation to generation.

Shepherd's Notes—Classics Series will help you take the first steps in claiming and drawing strength from your spiritual heritage.

Shepherd's Notes is designed to bridge the gap between now and then and to help you understand, love, and benefit from the company of saints of an earlier time. Each volume gives you an overview of the main themes dealt with by the author and then walks with you step-by-step through the classic.

Enjoy!
In Him,

David R. Shepherd
Editor-in-Chief

DESIGNED FOR THE BUSY USER

Shepherd's Notes for Calvin's *Institutes* is designed to provide an easy-to-use tool for gaining a quick overview of the major themes and the structure of *Institutes*.

Shepherd's Notes are designed for laymen, pastors, teachers, small-group leaders and participants, as well as the classroom student.

DESIGNED FOR QUICK ACCESS

Persons with time restraints will especially appreciate the timesaving features built into *Shepherd's Notes*. All features are designed to work together to aid a quick and profitable encounter with *Institutes*—to point the reader to sections in *Institutes* where they may want to spend more time and go deeper.

Book-at-a-Glance. Provides a listing of the major sections of the *Institutes*.

Summary. Each book of *Institutes* is summarized section by section.

Shepherd's Notes—Commentary. Following the summary of the book, a commentary is provided. This enables the reader to look back and see the major themes that make up that particular book.

Icons. Various icons in the margin provide information to help the reader better understand that part of the text. Icons include:

Shepherd's Notes Icon. This icon denotes the commentary section of each book of the *Institutes*.

Scripture Icon. Scripture verses often illuminate passages in *Institutes*.

Historical Background Icon. Many passages in *Institutes* are better understood in the light of historical, cultural, biographical, and geographical information.

Quotes Icon. This icon marks significant quotes from *Institutes*.

Points to Ponder Icon. These questions and suggestions for further thought will be especially useful in helping both individuals and groups see the relevance of *Institutes* for our time.

INTRODUCTION

BIBLIOGRAPHICAL AND HISTORICAL BACKGROUND

John Calvin was born in 1509 in the French town of Noyon, in Picardy (about 50 miles northeast of Paris), where his father held a position as a secretary for the bishop of the diocese. From a young age, Calvin was being groomed for the Catholic priesthood, having gained, through his father's influence, a chaplaincy at Noyon Cathedral when he was only eleven years old. This appointment made it possible for young John to receive an income from those who wished masses to be said at the cathedral. As was often the practice of the day, John's father hired a substitute to say mass in his place, since John was not yet old enough to be ordained a priest.

Soon after his appointment, he left Noyon to study Latin, logic, and philosophy at the University of Paris, receiving a Master of Arts degree at age seventeen. That same year his father sought to further Calvin's career in the church by obtaining two more church appointments, again hiring a substitute to carry out the daily duties of the parishes. But after coming into conflict with the bishop at Noyon, Calvin's father urged him to give up all thought of the priesthood and sent him to Orleans and later to Bourges to begin the study of law. After his father's death in 1531, Calvin moved back to Paris to continue his literary studies, returning only briefly to complete his law degree.

As a student, Calvin had frequent contact with those who had Protestant leanings, particularly his cousin Pierre (Olivetan) Robert, who himself

Calvin's cousin, Pierre Robert, went by the name *Olivetanus* or *Olivetan*. He came to be called *Olivetanus* because he burned the midnight oil. Since he is best known by the name *Olivetan*, he will be referred to this way throughout *Shepherd's Notes.*

Calvin was not quick to move to the teachings of the reformers: "Offended by the novelty, I lent an unwilling ear, and at first, I confess, strenuously and passionately resisted; for (such is the firmness or effrontery with which it is natural to men to persist in the course which they have once undertaken) it was with the greatest difficulty I was induced to confess that I had all my life long been in ignorance and error" (quoted in *Theology of the Reformers*).

Sudden Conversion

"But God subdued and made teachable a heart which, for my age, was far too hardened in such matters. Having received some foretaste and knowledge of true piety, I was inflamed with such a great desire to profit by it that, although I did not give up my other studies, I worked only slackly at them" (Preface to the *Commentary on the Psalms*).

translated the Bible into French shortly before the first edition of Calvin's *Institutes* was published. And while in Paris, Calvin attended secret Protestant meetings, despite what he referred to as his "obdurate attachment to papistical superstitions."

In 1532, Calvin received his Doctor of Laws degree and published his first book, a commentary, written in Latin, on one of Seneca's writings. Soon after this event he made a decisive break with the Roman Catholic Church, experiencing a (sparsely described) "sudden conversion" which impelled him on the mission of restoring the church to the purity of God's original intention. Though the exact date and details of this "conversion" are uncertain, by 1533, he had become one of the leading Protestant thinkers in Paris.

When Calvin's friend, Nicholas Cop, was elected rector of the University of Paris in 1533, it is believed that Calvin helped him write his inaugural address, which contained a strong attack on abuses in the church and an enthusiastic call for reform. This address stirred up such anti-Protestant sentiment that a warrant was issued for Cop's arrest by the city council and both Calvin and Cop fled from Paris.

During the next three years, Calvin was on the run, avoiding the anti-Protestant persecution of King Francis I, returning in 1534 to his hometown of Noyon, where he resigned his appointments with the church and seems to have been imprisoned for a time. After two hundred Protestants were arrested and twenty of them executed by a 1535 order of King Francis I, Calvin fled to the German city of Basel, which had recently become officially Protestant. Despite being on the run, Calvin focused his energies on creating written materials in support of the reformation cause.

In 1536, when Calvin was twenty-seven, the first (Latin) edition of *Institutes of the Christian Religion* was published. Calvin's original intent was to provide an elementary manual for understanding Protestant doctrine, particularly to be used as a tool for training Protestant ministers. This first edition was divided into six chapters: Law, Faith, Prayer, Sacraments, False Sacraments, Christian Liberty, and Church and State Authority. The book was enthusiastically received by Protestant theologians everywhere, including Luther.

Calvin returned to Paris briefly but soon fled to Basel, intending to find there the freedom necessary to direct his attention to a life of scholarship and writing. But to avoid the large army of King Francis amassed at the border of France and Germany, Calvin found himself, as if by accident, taking a detour through Switzerland, intending to spend just a single night in Geneva. This was a city which had, under the leadership of Protestant preacher, Guillaume Farel, revolted against its bishop and had embraced the cause of the Reformation.

With the movement in a state of tenuous disorder, Farel, having learned of the young scholar's presence in his city, insistently appealed to Calvin for assistance. When Calvin resisted on the grounds that he was a scholar and writer, not a Reformer, Farel threatened the curse of God on Calvin if he retreated from this urgent calling to a life of quiet scholarship. Calvin reluctantly agreed. In 1537, Calvin was

Calvin's preference was to work as a scholar in some secluded place, but God had other ideas. In your own life, has God called you to tasks that affirmed your preferences or placed you in situations that you wouldn't have chosen for yourself?

Final Words to Farel

"Since it is God's will that you should outlive me, remember our friendship. It was useful to God's Church and its fruits await us in heaven" (Calvin's last letter to William Farel).

appointed preacher (one of the city's three pastors) and professor of theology in Geneva.

Later in the same year, he and Farel drew up a set of ordinances to govern the churches and a confession of faith that the city council would eventually require all citizens to sign. Despite strong resistance from the citizens, by 1538, all had complied with the requirement. As Farel and Calvin pushed forward with additional reforms, it wasn't long before their efforts created such enemies against them that they were forced to leave the city.

Calvin briefly returned to Basel; but at the invitation of Martin Bucer, he moved to Strasbourg, an important imperial city in Germany. There he enjoyed perhaps the happiest three years of his ministry, working in relative tranquillity. He served as minister to French refugees in Strasbourg and married Idelette de Bure, a widow of an Anabaptist whom Calvin had led to the Reformed position. She bore him a son who died a few days after birth.

Calvin organized his Strasbourg ministry along the lines that he believed to be closest to the New Testament pattern, and he created a liturgy based on a French metrical translation of the book of Psalms. While in Strasbourg, he completed his commentary on Romans, published an enlarged version of the *Institutes* and its first French edition. In addition, he was also involved in gatherings with Lutheran and Roman Catholic theologians, all of which led to his increasing notoriety as a biblical scholar.

Despite his poor financial situation, Calvin would have been happy to remain in Strasbourg had it not been for the change in the political scene in Geneva. After Calvin's forced departure from Geneva, confusion and conflict reigned in the church. A Catholic cardinal named Sadoleto sought to bring the city once again under Roman control, but his effort had the opposite effect. The Genevans looked to Calvin for help in responding to pressure from Sadoleto, which resulted in Calvin's now famous Epistle to Cardinal Sadoleto, that vigorously defended the principles of the Reformation. After a change in the city government, which established supporters of Calvin in leadership, Calvin was convinced, after ten months of hesitation, to return in 1541.

He set immediately to the task of reforming the city that had become notorious for its immorality. He preached twice on each Sunday and once every Monday, Wednesday, and Friday, preaching verse by verse through whole books of the Bible, picking up at the exact place that he had left off his preaching there three years earlier.

Calvin labored to revise the city's laws, establish a form of church government, revise his psalter-based liturgy, and establish an academy to train the young. Calvin's vision of leading Geneva to become a theocracy was implemented through a series of "Ecclesiastical Ordinances," which established four classes of leadership in the church—pastors, doctors, elders, and deacons.

Church discipline was carried out by a "consistory" of ministers from all the churches in the city and twelve lay elders appointed by the town council The consistory, sometimes called the presbytery, met weekly to respond to issues related to the morality of its citizens, holding the power of excommunication of the unrepentant, whose offenses included wife beating, drunkenness, dancing, and gambling. But it was the town council, not the consistory, that held the power to mete out all other punishments.

His aim was to make Geneva a "holy city." As a result, he established strict, often harsh, discipline, of which most (even Calvinists) today would not approve. But the effect of his reforms was to create a dramatic change in the character of the city, bringing it significant notoriety throughout sixteenth-century Europe. Calvin held no official government position in Geneva and was not even a citizen until 1559. He exerted his influence by appointing pastors and by teaching and preaching.

Despite the positive changes in the city brought about by his reforms, Calvin still faced vigorous resistance in Geneva, sometimes resulting in riots and disturbances in the city, with his opponents hoping again to expel him from Geneva. In 1548, Calvin's opponents won a majority in the city council which they retained for several years. At this time, Calvin was also facing a long and severe struggle against a group referred to as the Libertines. When his popularity reached its lowest ebb, his wife died, leaving him to care for her two children from her previous marriage.

When the conflict was at its sharpest, in 1553, a Spaniard named Michael Servetus, arrived in Geneva, fleeing a death sentence for heresy in France. While attending one of Calvin's services, Servetus was recognized by Calvin and publicly condemned as a heretic. The city council, although at this time bitterly hostile to Calvin, arrested Servetus. Taking the trial completely out of Calvin's hands, the council, after consulting with a number of Swiss Protestant churches, came to a unanimous decision that

Servetus should be burned at the stake. Though Calvin agreed with the justice of the capital sentence, he did urge the council to substitute a milder form of execution, a request which they summarily denied.

By 1555, the resistance had been defeated, and Calvin was, until his death, recognized as the undisputed authority of the city. Calvin continued to move Geneva toward becoming a Christian commonwealth, revising its laws, establishing a universal system of education of the young, and founding systems for the intentional care of the poor and the aged.

Because Geneva was at a geographic crossroads, persecuted Protestants throughout Europe began to flock there. Under Calvin's influence, the city opened its gates to these refugees, who often returned home as missionaries for the cause of the Reformation. The establishment of the Geneva Academy in 1559 for the training of Protestant ministers provided an intentional forum for the dissemination of Reformed principles throughout Europe. Calvin's influence on the Protestant movement in France was immense, Geneva eventually becoming the chief source of pastors for French Protestant (or Huguenot) congregations.

In addition to his preaching, Calvin produced commentaries on twenty-three Old Testament books and on all books of the New Testament except the book of Revelation. He tirelessly produced pamphlets related to the cause of the Reformation. After Calvin's wife died, he suffered stomach ulcers and similar physical problems, as he, for the next fifteen years, gave himself relentlessly to his work. He died in 1564 at the relatively young age of 55 and at his

Did Calvin Have Servetus Burned?

"It is to him, notwithstanding, that men have always imputed the guilt of that funeral pire which he wished had never been reared" (Rilliet).

Final Words

"I have had many infirmities which you have been obliged to bear with, and what is more, all I have done has been worth nothing. . . . But certainly I can say this, that I have willed what is good, that my vices have always displeased me, and that the root of the fear of God has been in my heart; . . . and I pray you that the evil be forgiven me, and if there is any good, that you conform yourselves to it and make it an example" (Words to a gathering of pastors at Calvin's home, shortly before his death, quoted in Parker, *John Calvin*).

Imagine yourself close to death and having your last conversation with family and close friends. Would you find the substance of Calvin's last words appropriate for you as you depart? If not, what would you like your parting words to be?

request was buried in an unmarked grave in the cemetery of Geneva.

Though Calvin is often maligned as a cheerless legalist who labored to remove all joy from the Christian life, we have only to read his works or his letters to recognize how far this caricature is from the truth. Repeatedly in the *Institutes*, he wrote of the necessity of the engagement of the heart in matters of faith and the inherent joy and comfort of embracing the promises of the gospel.

In addition to his appreciation of poetry and music, Calvin's letters reveal many tender friendships. Though he admitted (and begged forgiveness for) his own impetuosity of temper, his sincere desire was to seek to understand the exact sense of the Scripture and then to submit to its authority.

FORMATIVE INFLUENCES

As Calvin was beginning his theological training, the Reformation was entering a second phase in its development. The changes brought about by Luther and other reformers not only introduced people to the Scripture in new ways, but they also resulted in immense and threatening changes in society at large. The removal of old restraints had given rise to speculations that threatened the moral standards and social order. Calvin responded, emphasizing in a chaotic environment, the priority of doing things "decently and in order" and thus giving definition to new forms of Christian living.

Though Calvin admitted that the Bible does not answer every question raised by human curiosity, his entire work breathes with the foundational assumption that the Scripture is the beginning and grounding point of all understanding of God. The *Institutes* is not a systematic theology in the contemporary sense but is best seen as a guide to the study of the Bible, pointing the reader to "what he ought especially to seek in Scripture, and to what end he ought to relate its contents."

Early in the sixteenth century, Ulrich Zwingli had begun preaching along Protestant lines in Switzerland, and Jacques Lefèvre d'Étaples was doing the same in France. In 1517, when Luther posted his 95 Theses on the door of the Wittenburg church, the small fires of reformation began to spread. It was into this environment that young John Calvin began his work as a Reformer.

The flavor of the *Institutes* was influenced largely by the persecution of Protestants in France. In this context, Calvin created a compelling defense for the Reformation position rather than a mere compendium of dogma. The original version, containing only six chapters, was published in 1536. After many revisions, the final publication in 1559 had grown to four books of seventy-nine chapters. This final edition is designed around a simple structure: Book One contains the doctrines related to the knowledge of God the Father; Book Two, the knowledge of God the Redeemer; Book Three, the work of the Holy Spirit; and Book Four, the doctrines related to the church.

It is obvious from even a cursory reading of the *Institutes* that no influence was as formative for Calvin's thinking as the Scriptures themselves. Before Calvin's conversion to the Reformation position, his kinsman, Olivetan, himself a future translator of the Bible into French, encouraged Calvin to study the Scripture for himself, an exhortation that Calvin obviously took to heart,

Jacques Lefèvre d'Étaples was known by two other names: *Jacobus Faber* and *Faber Stapulensis.*

When Luther died in 1546, the leadership of the Reformation passed to the second generation of leaders. The next year, when the German Protestant princes were defeated by the Catholic emperor, Geneva emerged as the leading city of the Protestant movement.

In each edition, the book begins with a preface addressed to Francis I, setting before that ruler a concise and clear request that his doctrines at least gain a hearing.

studying the Scriptures not only in Latin but in the original Greek and Hebrew as well. In addition, hardly a chapter goes by in the *Institutes* that Calvin does not refer back to the language and writings of Augustine. Next to Scripture, no other single influence was as formative for Calvin as Augustine.

IMPACT OF THE WORK

From the first edition, Calvin's *Institutes* was an epoch-making book. And apart from the countries where Lutheranism dominated, the *Institutes* became the determinative theology of the Reformation, laying the groundwork for much that would take place in the Protestant Reformation in the next four centuries.

"I could gladly and profitably set myself down and spend all the rest of my life just with Calvin" (Karl Barth, quoted in *Theology of the Reformers*).

The publication of the *Institutes* thrust Calvin into leadership among the Reformers because of its unparalleled way of explaining and clarifying the central Reformed doctrines of the day. For the reforming church to become established, a work the caliber of the *Institutes* was imperative. The *Institutes* gave strength to the Reformation by providing a compelling, clearly articulated alternative to medieval scholasticism. As a result, the *Institutes* were greeted with immense popularity, being almost immediately translated into the various European languages. Its impact is attested to by the fact that current translations of the work exist in modern French, Spanish, Italian, Dutch, German, English, Greek, Arabic, Japanese, and the language of Hungary.

"The masterpiece of Protestant theology"—Albrecht Ritschl's description of the *Institutes*.

Calvin's legacy through the *Institutes* goes far beyond those in the Reformed tradition. Calvin's precision and theological insight have provided all of Protestantism with a vocabulary for their own understanding of God, giving clarity to doctrines like the ultimate authority of

Scripture and justification by faith alone. Similarly, the doctrines of the Trinity, the person of Christ, atonement, and justification by faith are all teachings shared in common among all of Protestantism. Calvin's unique contribution was to present systematically these doctrines and place them beneath the overarching vision of the supreme power and glory of God.

Though the *Institutes* offered a profound, unified presentation of Reformed doctrine, little about Calvin's particular doctrines, taken by themselves, is unique to Calvin. Even the doctrine of predestination, which is often assumed to be peculiarly Calvinistic, is at least as old as Augustine, who intensely (and successfully) argued this doctrine against the Pelagians. In addition, this doctrine was held by Luther and Zwingli, the two other main figures in the Protestant Reformation.

Calvin's own doctrine of predestination is perhaps the most widely maligned and most oversimplified of all of Calvin's teachings. In contrast to England's Westminster Confession, which treats predestination at the beginning, Calvin does not develop his treatment of this doctrine until late in the third book (almost 1,000 pages into his work), as a corollary of what he had already demonstrated from Scripture about the nature of God's incomprehensible grace.

But it was not just the theology of the *Institutes* that made a lasting contribution. Calvin's ideas had and continue to have impact, far beyond the borders of Geneva, influencing Western thought concerning politics, science, and history in ways that were formative in the development of the entire Western culture and civilization in the modern era. And it has been

Pelagianism

Pelagius denied the total depravity of man. He believed that human beings were neutral at the outset, not tilted toward good or evil. He denied there was any difference between Adam and his posterity. He believed that good works could make a person right with God. The church eventually sided with Augustine. In the Western church, Pelagianism was condemned in 416 by the synods in Mileve and Carthage. In 418, the bishop of Rome took the same position. The Eastern Church condemned Pelagianism at the Counsel of Ephesus in 431.

said that the French translations of the *Institutes* had as great an influence on the development of the French language as it did on the Protestant movement in France.

As Protestants, like those fleeing the wrath of Catholic "bloody" Mary, fled to Geneva, they often returned to their own countries as Geneva-trained pastors, equipped with a systematic, orderly presentation of the Christian faith, which they used in the establishment of underground Protestant ministries. Puritanism in England, Republicanism in Holland, the Covenanting struggle in Scotland, and even the democratic institutions of America were all molded by the grand, logical, reformed thinking of John Calvin.

To what extent has John Calvin influenced your country? your church? you as a Christian?

PREFATORY ADDRESS TO KING FRANCIS

Calvin began the *Institutes* with a compelling appeal to the ruler of France, an appeal that clarified the primary purpose of the work and gave a fascinating inside look into the context in which Calvin's theology evolved. He began by affirming the immense hunger for Christ that he had observed among many of his countrymen in France. But since only a few of them had even a slight knowledge of Christ, Calvin's intention was to present the elementary teaching of Christian doctrine. But Calvin's fundamental appeal to the king was simply for a hearing. Calvin sought to arouse the king to cease the violence against Protestants, at least until he had given their doctrine a fair hearing to determine if it was biblical or a novel invention of misguided zealots.

Calvin then established the distinction between his doctrine and that of his opponents—the ruling Roman church. It all had to do, Calvin explained, with the fundamental understanding of the nature of God and the nature of humanity. Calvin's chief doctrine, which he emphasized over and over throughout his work, was that God is the sole author of all goodness and humanity is completely blinded by sin, unable, apart from grace, to ever know God.

"For they cannot bear that the whole praise and glory of all goodness, virtue, righteousness, and wisdom should rest with God" (Prefatory Address).

Calvin made sharp attacks on his opponents, declaring that their zeal for religion came not from a desire for truth but from a hunger for a full belly. He contrasted their indolent orthodoxy with those who laid down their lives for their doctrine.

Calvin refuted each attack from his opponents. To the accusation that the Protestant doctrine was "new," Calvin responded that nothing is new about the words of the Scripture. They are only new, Calvin maintained, to those who have never understood the gospel or Christ in the first place. To the accusation that the Protestant doctrine had not been attested to by miracles, he responded that Satan disguises himself as an angel of light (2 Cor. 11:14), and miracles can never be used to prove that a doctrine is true.

To the argument that the church fathers reject Reformation teaching, Calvin pointed out how often his opponents disagreed with the fathers of the church whenever it suited them. In almost poetic cadence, Calvin began each paragraph with a form of the question, "Was it not a father who said . . . ," citing at least ten specific teachings of the "fathers" that directly

Dung Amid Gold

"Their only care is to gather dung amid gold. . . . They . . . think that God is not rightly worshiped unless everything swims with untoward splendor, or, rather, mad excess" (Prefatory Address).

Spiritual Warfare

"Here is, as it were, a certain characteristic of the divine Word, that it never comes forth while Satan is at rest and sleeping. This is the surest and most trustworthy mark to distinguish it from lying doctrines" (Prefatory Address).

contradicted the accepted practices of the Roman church.

To the accusation that the Protestant doctrine was against custom, Calvin responded that a wrong custom does not cease to be wrong simply because the multitude practices it. To the argument that the Protestants were in error in their doctrine of the church, Calvin replied that the true church can never be fully equated with any visible representation of the church. Rather the mark of the true church is that it is the place where God's Word is purely preached and the sacraments are lawfully administered. Calvin rejected the notion that any human leader in the church can be said to speak without error, reminding the king that Aaron had been consecrated by the Lord but still led the Israelites into the error of worshiping the golden calf. And he condemned the equating of the church with "outward pomp," reminding his readers that the Pharisees involved themselves in similar external ceremonies.

To the accusation that Reformation teaching had created a tumult, Calvin explained that tumult and unrest often accompany the true proclamation of God's Word. He reminded his readers that Elijah, Christ, and the apostles were all considered seditious during their times, concluding with the challenge: Should the apostles have stopped proclaiming the gospel simply because it created unrest?

The final chapter of Calvin's preface begins with a bold warning to the king, promising that divine retribution awaits anyone responsible for torturing and condemning to death the innocent. Apologizing for the length of his preface, Calvin ended with a respectful appeal for the king to read the *Institutes* and make his own decision.

BOOK ONE: THE KNOWLEDGE OF GOD THE CREATOR

"The knowledge of ourselves not only arouses us to seek God, but also, as it were, leads us by the hand to find him. . . . Again, it is certain that man never achieves a clear knowledge of himself unless he has first looked upon God's face, and then descends from contemplating him to scrutinize himself" (I:I:1–2).

BOOK-AT-A-GLANCE

I–IV The Knowledge of God and the Knowledge of Self

V The Revelation of God

VI–IX The Role of Scripture

X–XII The Worship of God

XIII The Nature of God

XIV The Nature of Angels and Devils

XV The Nature of Humanity

XVI–XVIII The Providence of God

SUMMARY I–IV: THE KNOWLEDGE OF GOD AND THE KNOWLEDGE OF SELF

Calvin began his *Institutes* by asserting that the knowledge of God and the knowledge of self are inextricably bound together, that one cannot be had without the other. Calvin so linked the knowledge of God to love and reverence for God that "piety" is understood as a necessary prerequisite for any true understanding of God.

Piety

"I call 'piety' that reverence joined with love of God which the knowledge of his benefits induces. For until men recognize that they owe everything to God, . . . they will never yield him willing service. Nay, unless they establish their complete happiness in him, they will never give themselves truly and sincerely to him" (I:II:1).

15

God in My Own Image

"In seeking God, miserable men do not rise above themselves as they should, but measure him by the yardstick of their own carnal stupidity, and neglect sound investigation. . . . They do not therefore apprehend God as he offers himself, but imagine him as they have fashioned him in their own presumption" (I:IV:1).

"All men have a vague general veneration for God, but very few really reverence him; and wherever there is great ostentation in ceremonies, sincerity of heart is rare indeed" (I:II:2).

What did Calvin mean when he said that knowledge of self and knowledge of God are strongly interconnected? Read chapter 1 of the *Institutes*. How will people respond as they begin to know themselves by reference to God?

Calvin established clearly that although the knowledge of God is undeniably implanted in every person, still "all degenerate from the true knowledge of [God]." Though humans habitually create gods of their own making through superstition or presumption, belief in a god of one's own making, Calvin declared, must by no means be confused with a true knowledge of God.

COMMENTARY

Calvin's selection of his first topic for the *Institutes* says a great deal about his own perspective and priorities. While Calvin could have begun his work with a discussion of providence, or the authority of Scripture, or even predestination, he began with the knowledge of God. By this choice, he made clear from the outset that true knowledge of God is much more than mere mental assent or acceptance of orthodox propositions. Without using explicit contemporary terminology, Calvin was grounding his work in the fundamental assumption that the essence of true religion is a relationship with the only true God and that participation in religious ceremonies does not guarantee a true knowledge of God.

In these first few chapters, Calvin set the stage for his later reflections about the nature of humanity, as he colorfully described human blindness and humans' tendency toward self-delusion in spiritual things. Even in these early chapters, the reader can see Calvin's concern to show God's complete beneficence and the complete corruption of humans.

SUMMARY V: THE REVELATION OF GOD

Calvin declared that God is so obviously revealed through the created order that humans are without excuse in their rejection of God. After listing many evidences of the wisdom of God in creation, he described humans as a "microcosm" of God's workmanship, themselves the "loftiest proof" of God's wisdom. Calvin pointed not only to the evidences of God in creation but also to his providential ordering of events.

But, Calvin admitted, despite the powerful and compelling revelation of God in creation, humans consistently turn away from God, confusing the glory of the creation with the glory of the Creator. Though creation can awaken, arouse, and encourage humans to look toward God, such knowledge, in and of itself, is not sufficient to attain the true knowledge of God until the eyes have been "illumined by the inner revelation of God."

 COMMENTARY

In this chapter, Calvin did not focus his attention simply on the evidences of God in creation. His overriding theme was the blamelessness of God's fashioning the universe and the blameworthiness of humans who, through their own dullness, are unable to see God through creation.

Calvin affirmed repeatedly that creation gives humans enough knowledge of God to leave them without excuse in their rejection of God. He declared that humans fully deserve God's just punishment for their own dullness, even

Without Excuse

"But upon his individual works he has engraved unmistakable marks of his glory, so clear and so prominent that even unlettered and stupid folk cannot plead the excuse of ignorance. . . . Wherever you cast your eyes, there is no spot in the universe wherein you cannot discern at least some sparks of his glory. . . . This skillful ordering of the universe is for us a sort of mirror in which we can contemplate God, who is otherwise invisible" (I:V:1).

"But because most people, immersed in their own errors, are struck blind in such a dazzling theater, [the psalmist] exclaims that to weigh these works of God wisely is a matter of rare and singular wisdom. . . . And certainly however much the glory of God shines forth, scarcely one man in a hundred is a true spectator of it!" (I:V:8).

Inexcusable

"And where Paul teaches that what is to be known of God is made plain from the creation of the universe, he does not signify such a manifestation as men's discernment can comprehend; but, rather, shows it not to go farther than to render them inexcusable" (I:V:14).

What can you know about God from His creation?

Spectacles of Scripture

"Just as old or bleary-eyed men and those with weak vision, if you thrust before them a most beautiful volume, even if they recognize it to be some sort of writing, yet can scarcely construe two words, but with the aid of spectacles will begin to read distinctly; so Scripture, gathering up the otherwise confused knowledge of God in our minds, having dispersed our dullness, clearly shows us the true God" (I:VI:1).

though that revelation of nature is not sufficient to bring people to a saving knowledge of God.

SUMMARY VI–IX: THE ROLE OF SCRIPTURE

After acknowledging that the creation, in and of itself, is insufficient to bring about a saving knowledge of God, Calvin affirmed that God's revelation through Scripture is necessary for any true understanding of the Creator. But the Scripture's authority, he explained, is dependent not upon the judgment of the church but upon the confirming, illuminating work of the Holy Spirit. This leads to Calvin's foundational understanding that the Word and the Spirit, rightly understood, are held together by a "mutual bond."

 COMMENTARY

In a religious culture that has elevated a personal religious experience above sound doctrine based on Scripture, Calvin's attack on those who subordinate the Scripture to the revelation of the Spirit is astoundingly contemporary. His doctrine of the "mutual bond" between the Word and the Spirit provides a helpful corrective to the modern absurdity of those who make personal experience the final arbiter of truth.

SUMMARY X–XII: THE WORSHIP OF GOD

In chapter 10, Calvin briefly reaffirmed that the knowledge of God is revealed most "intimately" and "vividly" through the Scripture and that such knowledge is confirmed by a believer's experience of God. He concluded that all "heathen" are dragged into error through the "vague wanderings of their minds" and are inexcusable in their rejection of God.

In chapter 11, Calvin condemned the use of images in worship, claiming that the use of images reduces God's glory to vain imagination of "earthly manikins" (humans). Beginning his arguments from the prohibition of images for God in the Ten Commandments, Calvin argued that all images for God, as expressions of human speculation, simply feed the human hunger for visible idols. Though he affirmed that art is God's good gift, Calvin condemned the use of images in worship by the Roman church.

In chapter 12, Calvin declared that true honoring of God requires that no observance of piety (such as praying to an image or to a saint) be transferred from God to another. Whenever such honor is bestowed upon a part of creation (e.g., the sun or the moon) or an image (whether of God or His saints), that honor is removed from God.

 COMMENTARY

In Chapter 11, Calvin made his first direct attack on the "papists" (the Roman Catholic Church). His attack comes in the form of his characteristic style of debate, arguing first from Scripture and then from the history of the church, using the Scripture as the lens for judging all conclusions of the church or earlier theologians. Both here and throughout the *Institutes*, Calvin depended heavily on Augustine's writings to support his own views.

SUMMARY XIII: THE NATURE OF GOD

Calvin defined and defended the doctrine of the Trinity, namely that God is a single, undivided

Word and Spirit

"Therefore Scripture will ultimately suffice for a saving knowledge of God only when its certainty is founded upon the inward persuasion of the Holy Spirit. . . . But those who wish to prove to unbelievers that Scripture is the Word of God are acting foolishly, for only by faith can this be known" (I:VIII:13).

What two kinds of undesirable consequences result when the "mutual bond" of Scripture and the Spirit is not observed?

Vain Speculation

"All we conceive concerning God in our own minds is an insipid fiction" (I:XI:4).

Why do we humans have a preference for constructing God in our likeness rather than receiving God's self-revelation?

Both God and Father

"'Christ with respect to himself is called God; with respect to the Father, Son. Again, the Father with respect to himself is called God; with respect to the Son, Father'" (Augustine I:XIII:19).

essence in the three persons of the Father, the Son, and the Holy Spir˙. He argued that this understanding of God is so fundamental that without this understanding, the knowledge of God is reduced to a "bare and empty name" that "flits about in our brains." Calvin admitted that although the Scriptures themselves never use the explicit term "*Trinity*" in referring to God, ample evidence can be found in Scripture to confirm conclusively both the unity of God's essence and the Trinity of God's persons.

Acknowledging that the severe "poverty of human speech" makes it impossible to describe God perfectly, Calvin seeks to spend little time haggling over the variety of words that have been used to explain the Trinity. Rather than "essence" and "person," Calvin chooses instead to speak of God as having one "substance" containing three "subsistences." He explained that though each person of the Trinity cannot be separated from the substance of the Godhead, they can be distinguished from it. And though there is a natural sequence from the Father to the Son and from the Father and the Son to the Spirit, each subsistence of God is equally God.

Using extensive scriptural proofs, Calvin affirmed the deity of each person of the Trinity. He worked to harmonize the opinions of ancient writers under the fundamental rubric of God's one essence and three persons, admitting that they often seem to contradict one another and even themselves. He refuted the ancient (Arius, Sabellius) and contemporary (Servetus) heresies that rejected the orthodox doctrine of the Trinity, particularly condemning those who taught that only the Father is properly God. He concluded the chapter with a powerful argument from historical precedent that all the "doctors" of the church agree on the fundamental doctrine of the Trinity.

COMMENTARY

Chapter 13 expresses Calvin's foundational understanding of the nature of God. This chapter sets the stage for Calvin's sequential reflection on the nature of each person of the Trinity, beginning his discussion of God the Father in the next chapter (14), God the Son in Book 2 (particularly ch. 6ff.), and God the Holy Spirit in Book 3 (ch. 1ff.).

Though Calvin was a brilliant wordsmith, he urged great caution and moderation in words used to express the nature of God, acutely aware of the severe limitation of words in penetrating to the nature of God. And though he examined extensively this doctrine of the Trinity, he returned again and again to the simple affirmation that God is one in essence and comprehended in three persons. Though Calvin clung to the Scripture as the foundation of all that he had to say about the Trinity, he did not accept the dead literalism of those who rejected the use of the word "*Trinity*" because the Bible does not expressly use that vocabulary.

Calvin hinted at the purpose of his work when he explained that his primary goal was not to convince those who are "inflexible and contentious" but "those who are teachable." Though the *Institutes* contain strong arguments against Calvin's opponents, the *Institutes* is best understood not as a direct argument with his opponents but as a tool for equipping others to be well prepared for encountering such opponents.

Ancient Heresies

Arius (d-337) taught that Christ was not equal to the Father but was created by the Father for the salvation of humankind. Sabellius (250) believed that the Father, Son, and Holy Spirit were not different persons subsisting in one God but simply diverse attributes for God.

Scripture doesn't use the word *Trinity*. Why is the doctrine of the Trinity so important to Calvin?

**The Nicene Creed
(4th century A.D.)**

We believe in one God the Father Almighty, Maker of heaven and earth, and of all things visible and invisible.

SUMMARY XIV: THE NATURE OF ANGELS AND DEVILS

The heart of this chapter contains Calvin's biblical reflections on the nature of angels, arguing that they are not mere ideas but actualities. The creation of angels, he explained, is not included in the biblical creation account because it tells only of those created things visible to the eyes. But, he argued, the evidence from Scripture is so explicit that the believer can obtain some understanding of angels and devils, though Scripture remains silent about those things that feed only the curiosity.

Calvin explained that the Scripture fundamentally teaches that angels are God's ministers, "celestial spirits" carrying out God's decrees. The Scripture sometimes describes them as winged creatures, a reminder to believers of the swiftness with which they are prepared to render aid. But Calvin rejected the notion of each person having his or her own guardian angel as an unbiblical idea.

Calvin summarized Scripture's teaching on the nature of devils: They were created as angels of God, who rebelled, resulting in their own ruin, becoming "instruments of ruin for others." He declared that "the devil" is in no way an equal opposite of God but rather, part of God's creation. He identified a single, fundamental purpose of all scriptural teaching concerning devils—to arouse God's people to be prepared for battle against this adversary.

 COMMENTARY

In speaking of evil's origin, Calvin offered his characteristic, delicate argument, affirming the blamelessness of God and the blameworthiness of His creation. While clearly declaring the devil's responsibility for his own perversion and "deliberate opposition to God," Calvin also asserted (based on Scripture) that the devil himself is an instrument of God, whose every action is subject to God's bidding and "dependent upon God's sufferance." Calvin suggested that God uses even the unclean spirits to "exercise" believers, but never to "vanquish or crush them."

Calvin's discussion of angels and devils is bracketed in this chapter by affirmations of the goodness of God's creation. This context implies that angels and devils should also be understood as gifts of creation, examples of God's provision to awaken God's people.

What is the role of angels? What is the origin of the devil and his angels?

SUMMARY XV: THE NATURE OF HUMANITY

Calvin presented a twofold description of human nature: first, that humans "proceeded spotless from God's hand" as God's most remarkable work; and second, that the image of God, though still present in all humans, has nearly been obliterated through the Fall. Calvin described the remnant of God's image in humans as "confused, mutilated, and disease-ridden," and "almost blotted out" by Adam's defection from God. But God supplied the remedy for this condition in the regenerative work of Christ, through which God's image is restored in believers.

Know Thyself

"We cannot have a clear and complete knowledge of God unless it is accompanied by a corresponding knowledge of ourselves" (I:XV:1, p. 183).

He draws a distinction between the human soul (or spirit) and human body, referring to the former as the "nobler part" which arouses men to honor God. Calvin divides all faculties of soul into the two broad categories of "understanding" and "will," offering a critique of the opinions of various philosophers concerning the soul.

COMMENTARY

Calvin's language at the beginning of this chapter harks back to the first lines of the *Institutes*, as he described the indispensable need of believers to understand themselves if they are to understand God clearly. In typical fashion, he anticipated the most likely question his readers might have: Why did God not make Adam in such a way that he would not desire to sin? Calvin responded simply that God's secret purposes are beyond human understanding.

What did Adam's sin do to the image of God in human beings?

SUMMARY XVI–XVIII: THE PROVIDENCE OF GOD

In chapter 16, Calvin argued that a proper understanding of God the Creator includes the recognition of God's ongoing work in creation. He intensely resisted the idea that God was simply a "momentary Creator," finishing His active work in the world at the end of the seven days of creation. He rejected the idea of fortune, chance, or fate, arguing that all events, whether in nature or in human experience, are "governed by God's secret plan." Calvin renounced the idea that God's omnipotence is idle or uninvolved, insisting rather that God is actively engaged moment by moment in the details of the governance of His creation.

"Are not two sparrows sold for a penny? Yet not one of them will fall to the ground apart from the will of your Father" (Matt. 10:29).

A proper understanding of the providence of God, according to Calvin, leads believers to a certainty of God's unassailable protection. Though God is the ultimate cause of all events,

Calvin suggested that the specific reason for specific occurrences remain hidden in the mind of God, far above human understanding.

In chapter 17, Calvin explained how believers may fruitfully profit from the doctrine of providence. He suggested that this doctrine leads to a wholehearted respect for God, whose wisdom is far beyond human understanding and prevents believers from arrogantly demanding God to render account for His actions.

Calvin explained that, though God governs every detail of human life by His providence, humans are not thereby excused from responsibility. Calvin renounced the shallow arguments of those who assume that a belief in providence shifts the blame for all wickedness from the evildoer onto the "naked providence of God." Calvin sought to clarify that though God, in His boundless wisdom, is able to use evil actions for His own purposes, those who commit wickedness remain without excuse before God. Though Calvin admitted that God uses the evil intent of the wicked, still such wickedness finds its source not in God but in humans.

Calvin declared that believers experience a unique happiness when they rightly recognize God's providential hand, seeing God's diligent care for the details of the lives of His children, God's abundant provision in prosperity, the availability of God's help in adversity. Those who fully embrace the doctrine of providence, said Calvin, experience the "immeasurable felicity of the godly mind," but those who do not understand God's providence can never place their full confidence in God.

Calvin, aware of his opponents, briefly considered those scriptural passages where God is

God's Reasons

"God always has the best reason for his plan. . . . Yet however hidden and fugitive from our point of view the causes may be, we must hold that they are surely laid up with him" (XVII:1).

"Oh, the depth of the riches of the wisdom and knowledge of God! How unsearchable his judgments, and his paths beyond tracing out!" (Rom. 11:33).

Providence

"If you pay attention, you will easily perceive that ignorance of providence is the ultimate of all miseries; the highest blessedness lies in the knowledge of it" (I:XVII:11).

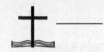

"He who is the Glory of Israel does not lie or change his mind; for he is not a man, that he should change his mind" (1 Sam. 15:29).

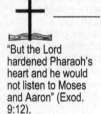

"But the Lord hardened Pharaoh's heart and he would not listen to Moses and Aaron" (Exod. 9:12).

described as "repenting." Calvin explained that each time the Scripture speaks of God's "repentance," it is only to make allowance for the dullness of human understanding. Even in those places in which Scripture appears to portray God as changing His mind, Calvin's understanding, based on the overwhelming evidence throughout the Scripture, is that God's plan and will are never reversed, no matter how sudden the change may appear to human eyes.

In chapter 18, Calvin concluded book one with the logical conclusion of his doctrine of providence—that God, in His boundless wisdom, is able to use the evil works of the ungodly, "bending their minds to carry out his judgments," but in such a way as to leave God blameless. Examining an extensive selection of texts from Scripture, Calvin affirmed that, though evil men or Satan may instigate wickedness, God holds the key and they can do nothing unless God turns the key. Calvin resisted limiting God's role to mere "permission," affirming that nothing happens that is outside God's eternal decrees.

 COMMENTARY

In earlier editions of the *Institutes*, Calvin included his discussions of providence and predestination in the same section. But in his final edition, he postponed his discussion of predestination until Book 3, including it in his discussion of the work of the Holy Spirit.

The modern reader may easily take offense at Calvin's doctrine of God's providence. Calvin's understanding of the nature of God is radically different from the commonly held view of the "clockmaker god," who set the world in motion, established its laws, and then remains passively at a distance. Of course, the harshest implication of this doctrine is its inference that every event—the death of a child, the genocide of a nation, the rape of the helpless—occurs under the authority of God's providential care. Many choose to believe in a God who might be less involved in the universe and perhaps less able to render aid in order to avoid believing that God would ever allow evil to occur. Calvin's argument is that humans dare not postulate a God of their liking but rather must seek to know the God who has revealed Himself in the Scriptures.

COMMENTARY

Though belief in the doctrine of providence has sometimes been perceived as a belief in a cold, capricious God who is the cause of every tragedy, Calvin suggested that this doctrine, when rightly perceived, brings inestimable comfort to the believer. In times of affliction, those who rightly understand the providence of God can rest in the certainty that they are held securely in God's hands, suffering nothing except what their loving Father has not only allowed but commanded.

BOOK TWO: THE KNOWLEDGE OF GOD THE REDEEMER IN CHRIST

If This Seems Harsh

"Let those for whom this seems harsh consider for a little while how bearable their squeamishness is in refusing a thing attested by clear Scriptural proofs because it exceeds their mental capacity. . . . For our wisdom ought to be nothing else than to embrace with humble teachableness, and at least without finding fault, whatever is taught in Sacred Scripture" (I:XVIII:4).

Surprised?

Though Calvin wrote with intensity about the topic of providence, the reader will likely "look in vain to find the noun 'sovereignty' applied to God in Calvin's writings" (I:XIII:1, footnote 1).

After discussing the nature and work of God the Creator (or God the Father) in Book 1, Calvin continued, in logical progression, to discuss the

Self-Knowledge

"Know thyself" (inscription on the temple at Delphi).

nature and work of God the Redeemer (or God the Son) in Book 2. In neither book did Calvin focus on a cold, speculative knowledge of God. Instead, he linked the true knowledge of God with the true knowledge of self, beginning Book 2 by focusing on the fallen condition of humanity. Calvin then demonstrated how the Old Testament points to Christ, explaining in this context, the nature and purpose of the Law. After comparing the unity and distinctiveness of the Old and New Testaments, Calvin described the nature and purpose of Christ and Christ's work as Mediator on behalf of humankind.

BOOK-AT-A-GLANCE

I–VI The Corruption of Human Nature

VII–IX The Purpose of the Law (Including the Explanation of the Ten Commandments)

X–XI The Similarity and Distinctiveness of the Old and New Testaments

XII–XIV The Nature of Christ

XV–XVII The Work of Christ (Including the Explanation of the Apostle's Creed)

SUMMARY I: MAN'S FALL

Born in Sin

"Surely I was sinful at birth, sinful from the time my mother conceived me" (Ps. 51:5).
"Therefore, just as sin entered the world through one man, and death through sin, and in this way death came to all men" (Rom. 5:12).
"Like the rest, we were by nature objects of wrath" (Eph. 2:3).

Calvin reasserted that a proper knowledge of human nature is twofold: First, it contemplates the original endowment given to Adam at Creation; and second, it acknowledges the miserable condition of humanity after Adam's Fall. These two conditions are so linked together that, Calvin suggested, one cannot properly consider the "primal worthiness" of Adam without the "sorry spectacle of our foulness" also coming to mind. Despite the popular appeal of those who delude their listeners into self-admiration, a true knowledge of self, according to Calvin, always deprives humans of any ground for boasting.

Calvin drew a distinction between Adam's "first sin" which brought about the Fall and "original sin" which Calvin describes as the "inherited corruption" which deprives all humans of Adam's upright nature. Calvin affirmed that Adam's sin infected all who came after Adam with the "disease of sin," clarifying that even children of believers are born in sin, that no part of human nature is free from the corruption of sin.

COMMENTARY

Calvin seemed aware that the doctrine of original sin would meet resistance on the part of many of his readers. He therefore made his case through extensive references to Scripture, bringing Scripture to bear against the human tendency toward delusion and self-admiration.

Calvin took care to affirm that sin is not the natural endowment given to human beings at creation but is the corruption of that nature. Consistent with his emphasis throughout the *Institutes*, Calvin was cautious to ensure that his readers understood that God is not to blame for the fallenness of humanity.

SUMMARY II: FREE WILL

Calvin began this chapter by identifying the two most common dangers of misunderstanding the human condition: (1) If humans see themselves as totally devoid of uprightness, they can easily become complacent. (2) If people see the source of their goodness in themselves, they deprive God of honor by brazenly assuming credit for themselves. Calvin recommended a course between these two perils.

An Old Controversy

Pelagius, who opposed Augustine's doctrine of the complete depravity of humans, affirmed the natural moral ability of humankind. The historical orthodoxy of Calvin's teachings on original sin are supported by the fact that the teachings of Pelagius were condemned as heretical repeatedly by a variety of fifth-century church councils.

Why Didn't God . . .

"Let no one grumble here that God could have provided better for our salvation if he had forestalled Adam's fall. Pious minds ought to loathe this objection, because it manifests inordinate curiosity" (II:I:10).

What would Calvin say to those who ask why God didn't prevent Adam from sinning?

Who Were the Scholastics?

Scholasticism is a system of philosophy and theology begun in the twelfth and thirteenth centuries that applied Aristotle's categories to Christian revelation in an attempt to integrate philosophy and theology, reason and faith. Peter Lombard is the most quoted of the Scholastics in the *Institutes.*

Free Will

"Again, man, using free will badly, has lost both himself and his will. . . . Again, what God's grace has not freed will not be free" (II:II:8).

He offered a critique of the opinion of human nature offered by philosophers who affirmed the total freedom of the will and accepted reason as a sufficient guide for all human conduct. He noted the lack of consistency among both philosophers and church fathers. In his characteristic concurrence with Augustine, Calvin affirmed that free will is totally impossible without the assistance of grace. He rejected the teachings of the scholastic theologians who imply that humans, by their own nature, can somehow seek after good.

Calvin made a distinction between the words *"compulsion"* and *"necessity."* God does not, Calvin asserted, force humans to sin by some sort of "compulsion." Rather, all of them choose to sin out of their own wicked wills.

Calvin explained that because human nature is completely sinful, all people, by the very fact that they are human, sin out of "necessity," though at the same time they always do so voluntarily. In this sense, Calvin did assert a belief in "free will," which, for Calvin, amounted not to a human's natural ability to choose what is good but to his voluntary choice to do what is evil. Because of the fallenness of human nature, the only freedom of the human will, apart from grace, is the freedom *from* righteousness.

Calvin rejected any attempt to parcel out credit for good works between God and humans, warning against the danger of robbing God of honor through a false doctrine of the free will. Inviting his readers to look at themselves in the "faithful mirror of Scripture," Calvin recalled the devil's self-image-building words in the garden that first tempted man and woman to exalt themselves ("you will be like God," Gen. 3:5, NIV). Calvin affirmed the foundational principle that a true knowledge of oneself begins with the knowledge of one's absolute poverty before God.

Calvin then described the pervasive results of original sin—completely destroying all supernatural qualities (such as faith, love for God, and zeal for holiness) and corrupting and weakening the natural qualities of the reason and the will. Therefore, according to Calvin, despite the fact that a longing for eternal things is implanted in every human, the weakness and corruption of the will prevents them from steadfastly pursuing the truth of God. Calvin affirmed that the mind maintains the imprint of basic principles of right and wrong and of fair dealings.

Recognizing human accomplishment in the arts and science as a demonstration that human reason was not completely destroyed in the Fall, Calvin affirmed that any discovery of genuine truth finds its source in God. But he quickly added that all understanding of these matters is transitory and futile if it is not undergirded by the solid foundation of God's truth. Calvin also found in reason the distinguishing marks that separate humans from beasts and recognized in these marks "some remaining traces of the image of God."

Though he admitted that the power of human reason remains even in the ungodly, he hastened to clarify that spiritual discernment exists only in those who have been regenerated by Christ. When it comes to spiritual insight, Calvin declared, "the greatest geniuses are blinder than moles!" He explained that the

The Knowledge of God

"No one can come to me unless the Father who sent me draws him" (John 6:44). "The man without the Spirit does not accept the things that come from the Spirit of God, for they are foolishness to him, and he cannot understand them, because they are spiritually discerned" (1 Cor. 2:14).

Wholly Evil

"The LORD smelled the pleasing aroma and said in his heart: 'Never again will I curse the ground because of man, even though every inclination of his heart is evil from childhood'" (Gen. 8:21).

All from God

"'Confess that you have all things from God: whatever good you have is from him; whatever evil, from yourself'" (Augustine, II:II:27).

"Apart from me you can do nothing" (John 15:5).

spiritual blindness of humans is so great that they can have no knowledge of God unless the Spirit of God enlightens them.

Calvin explained that the natural law implanted in every human offers just enough truth to render him inexcusable before God, arguing that human knowledge will always fail to lead people to obey and worship God. Calvin taught that even the regenerate must depend on the Holy Spirit daily to lead them to a right knowledge of God.

 COMMENTARY

Though many, both ancient and modern, perceive Calvin's doctrine of the bondage of the will as unnecessarily negative, Calvin's primary concern was that believers recognize their absolute dependence on God. Though Calvin's doctrine may be criticized from a psychological point of view, it is difficult to argue with the case he made from Scripture.

As long as Calvin was allowed to use his own narrow definition of free will, namely that humans are free to choose evil but are free to choose good only by God's grace, he admitted that "free will" is an acceptable doctrine. But because the mere mention of the term "*free will*" almost always leads people to the false belief in their own power to choose what they can only choose by God's grace, Calvin argued that the church would be better off to abolish the use of the term altogether.

As opposed to those who argue that Christians can learn nothing from those who are not themselves believers, Calvin affirmed that much can be gained from the learned accomplishments of even the unregenerate. But he refused to give an uncritical acceptance to their conclusions, emphasizing that their powers of reason are limited because of their fallen nature.

SUMMARY III: CORRUPTED HUMAN NATURE

Calvin described the human condition in such a way as to declare all humans completely dependent on God's grace, requiring a total renewal of the mind and will. Turning to the "clear mirror" of Romans 3, Calvin declared the total corruption of the human condition, acknowledging the foolishness of seeking anything good from unredeemed human nature.

He explained that though God sometimes restrains humans from wickedness, even this restraint is a gift of God and is no argument for the natural human goodness. Though God sometimes may endow those destined for leadership with special gifts of heroism, Calvin argued that such gifts are evidence of God's special grace, not of human worthiness.

He delicately explained how it is possible that people sin both of necessity and freely. He affirmed that people sin by necessity, since human nature is so bent that all people (unless restrained or regenerated) will always choose evil. But at the same time, he clarified that when people choose to do wrong, they do so willingly—not unwillingly—making themselves voluntary slaves of the evil they choose.

The complete inability of humans to do good is seen, Calvin declared, most clearly in redemption, exclusively the work of God, beginning with God's arousing in believers a desire for righteousness and ending with God's granting His saints perseverance. Calvin, following the

"But if the Lord has willed that we be helped in physics, dialectic, mathematics, and other like disciplines, by the work and ministry of the ungodly, let us use this assistance. For if we neglect God's gift freely offered in these arts, we ought to suffer just punishment for our sloths" (II:II:16).

In what sense did Calvin allow that humans have free will?

No One

"There is no one righteous, not even one; there is no one who understands, no one who seeks God. All have turned away, they have together become worthless; there is no one who does good, not even one" (Rom. 3:10–12; cp. Ps. 14:3).

33

"For it is God who works in you to will and to act according to his good purpose" (Phil. 2:13).

Bidding Farewell to Works

"Yet there is nothing that we are more unwilling to do than to bid farewell to our own labors and to give God's works their rightful place" (II:III:9).

clear outlines of Scripture, emphasized that the credit for redemption must not be divided between humans and God; rather, he credited God exclusively for His transforming work in believers. From the first impulse to seek God, all credit for human good works belongs only to God, said Calvin.

Calvin rejected the notion that believers somehow "cooperate" with grace, as if something that humans do might motivate God to be gracious. God is always the one who acts first, according to Calvin, and what humans do in response to God comes about only because God has first acted upon the human will to make it responsive.

Calvin rejected as well the notion that God is merely extending His hand, waiting for humans to respond. Instead he argued that God's work in redemption is efficacious from beginning to end, not through cooperation with human response, but coming before and inspiring every human response. Calvin rejected any suggestion of a partnership in the work of humans and the work of God's grace, insisting that every human response to God is nothing more than a gift of God's grace. Leaning on the writings of Augustine, Calvin affirmed that God's initiative does not eliminate human will but simply makes that will totally dependent on God's grace.

 COMMENTARY

Against those who may rationalize their sin before God, considering themselves "not as bad as a lot of people," Calvin applied an impressive array of "thunderbolts" of Scripture, emphasizing the universality of the corruption of human nature. Despite the surface negativity of this doctrine, to Calvin such an understanding is essentially good news, since an accurate understanding of oneself is essential to a true knowledge of God.

As opposed to Calvin, some modern evangelicals maintain a fuzzy, confused notion of God's grace, thanking God for His complete grace in all areas of their lives, but at the same time assuming some sort of partnership with God in which God does His part and they do their part. In stark contrast, Calvin would affirm that the only one who has a part in the drama of salvation is God.

The implication of Calvin's teaching about humans' complete dependence on God's grace is that no one is saved because they are good enough, or smart enough, or prudent enough to choose God. According to Calvin (and, he would say, according to the Scriptures), no human left to himself or herself will ever choose God, since the desire to choose God is a gift, that takes away all room for human boasting.

SUMMARY IV: GOD'S WORK IN HUMAN HEARTS

Calvin affirmed that all humans find themselves naturally under the dominion of Satan and that all who are not rescued by God's gracious actions are abandoned to Satan's control. Admitting that Satan himself is nothing other than a minister of wrath, Calvin explained that though Scripture sometimes attributes the same work to God, Satan, and humans, it does so in such a way as to leave Satan and humans inexcusable and God blameless. Against those who seek a somewhat softer understanding of God's providence, Calvin argued that God's

Everyone Who Seeks Finds

"Men indeed ought to be taught that God's loving-kindness is set forth to all who seek it, without exception. But since it is those on whom heavenly grace has breathed who at length begin to seek after it, they should not claim for themselves the slightest part of his praise" (II:III:10).

"For it is by grace you have been saved, through faith—and this not from yourselves, it is the gift of God—not by works, so that no one can boast" (Eph. 2:8–9).

Some writers distinguish between God's part in salvation and our part. What is Calvin's view of this distinction?

Satan Serves God

"Yet in the same work there is always a great difference between what the Lord does and what Satan and the wicked try to do. God makes these evil instruments, which he holds under his hand and can turn wherever he pleases, to serve his justice" (II:IV:5).

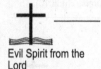

Evil Spirit from the Lord

"Now the Spirit of the Lord had departed from Saul, and an evil spirit from the Lord tormented him" (1 Sam. 16:14).

Reward

"'God does not crown our merits but his own gifts. . . . If you shall be paid what you deserve, you must be punished'" (Augustine II:V:2).

providence goes beyond a mere permission of evil, since God destines everything according to His own purposes.

Calvin affirmed that in every human decision, God's prompting and dominion stand above human freedom. He argued that the fact that humans are often able to accomplish what they choose does not in any way prove that humans are somehow at times free of God's rule.

 COMMENTARY

In this chapter, Calvin offered explanation for the troubling passages that might lead some to believe that Scripture teaches that God is somehow responsible for evil. Calvin established a creative tension between God's providence and God's goodness.

SUMMARY V: DEFENDERS OF FREE WILL

Calvin began the chapter by responding to common objections raised by the proponents of free will.

Calvin concluded the chapter by giving his rebuttal to a variety of proof texts used by the defenders of free will.

 COMMENTARY

One quality that makes the *Institutes* such fascinating reading is that Calvin was able to summarize succinctly and clearly the arguments of his opponents in such a way that those arguments are, at least at first glance, convincing. Then Calvin developed his masterful arguments, beginning typically with Scripture but

Common Objections	Calvin's Response
1. If humans sin of necessity, what they are doing cannot properly be called sin; if they sin voluntarily, they must have free will.	Beginning with Augustine's argument against the Pelagians, Calvin argued that although humans sin of necessity, they also willingly choose to sin voluntarily.
2. If sin is necessary, the concepts of reward and punishment and of good and evil become meaningless.	Since humans sin voluntarily, punishment is a meaningful consequence. Election and good works are gifts of God that God does indeed reward, making a clear distinction between good and evil.
3. If there were no free will, it would be meaningless to exhort people to do good.	Augustine, Christ, the apostles, Moses, and the prophets are all examples of those who offered exhortation to righteousness but who, at the same time, affirmed the bondage of humans to sin. Exhortation prepares believers for grace, and exhortation renders unbelievers inexcusable at the judgment.
4. Why would God give commands, promises, and reproofs if humans were unable to obey?	Scripture repeatedly teaches that the law is without effect unless the grace of God gives the power to obey. God's promises and reproofs prick the consciences of unbelievers, rendering them inexcusable. God's promises and reproofs awaken believers to the sweetness of God's precepts, arousing them to seek God's grace.
5. When God is described as waiting on human response, the Scripture clearly implies the freedom of the will.	God sometimes removes His presence and His Word from people that they might recognize their own need for God and, in their affliction, turn to seek Him.
6. Scripture often attributes good works to humans.	When Jesus said to pray for "our" daily bread, He was not implying that because it is ours it is not a gift of God. Likewise, simply because God works through human instrumentality does not mean that God is not the author of every good work.

Human Strength?

"'God bids us do what we cannot, that we may know what we ought to seek from him'" (Augustine IIV:7).

No Puppets

"Man's action is not taken away by the movement of the Holy Spirit" (II:V14).

The Foolishness of Mixing Free Will with Grace

"For any mixture of the power of free will that men strive to mingle with God's grace is nothing but a corruption of grace. It is just as if one were to dilute wine with muddy, bitter water" (II:V:15).

What did Calvin mean in saying that sin is both necessary and voluntary?

relying heavily on the writings of Augustine. By identifying his opponents' arguments with those of Augustine's old opponents, the Pelagians (views which were repeatedly condemned as heretical), he brought to bear not only the force of the Scripture but also that of the tradition of the church. Throughout the *Institutes*, he took great care to show that he was not creating a new or novel theology but simply asserting what had been the essence of orthodox Christian belief.

This chapter also clarifies Calvin's understanding of free will. Though he had said previously that he did not like the term because of its potential for confusing believers, in the strictest sense, Calvin did believe in the freedom of the human will. Humans, according to Calvin, freely and voluntarily choose evil and are thus responsible for those choices. Though their sin is necessary, it is no less voluntary. This voluntary sin is the essence of free will. Calvin, of course, would be quick to clarify that any human attempt to choose God does not come from free will but from God's grace.

SUMMARY VI: CHRIST, THE ONLY WAY TO SALVATION

Calvin affirmed that Christ, the Mediator, is the "only door" to a true knowledge of God and that those who do not look to Christ cannot worship in a way that pleases God. It is only those, Calvin explained, who have been engrafted into the body of Christ who can be called God's children.

Calvin explained that God never showed favor to His ancient people apart from the Mediator. Appealing to a variety of promises in the Old Testament, Calvin made the case that those who had faith in God under the old covenant did so through the promised Mediator, in that Christ was the "seed in which all the nations of the world were to be blessed" (see Gal. 3:14). He suggested that wherever hope is promised in the old covenant, Christ is prefigured and the godly in the Old Testament believed in Christ, even before He was born.

COMMENTARY

Throughout the *Institutes*, Calvin often referred to God's people before Christ as "the church." His emphasis was clear: The gospel comes before the Law, and the good news before the commandments.

Calvin was clear in this chapter that Christ is the only way to salvation, arguing that from the beginning of the world Christ was set before those whom God had elected to salvation. In response to the modern question, What about sincere people from other religions? Calvin would likely answer that those who embrace God the Creator while rejecting Christ the Mediator have substituted an idol for the true God.

SUMMARY VII: THE PURPOSE OF THE LAW: FOSTERING HOPE OF SALVATION IN CHRIST

In this chapter, Calvin explained that the Law was given for the primary purpose of instilling in God's people the hope for salvation in Christ. Starting from the promise given to Abraham four hundred years before the Law was given, Calvin asserted that the ceremonial laws of the old covenant were shadows and figures of the clear revelation of the gospel. He described the priesthood of the tribe of Levi and the royal line

Too Lofty without the Mediator

"Although faith rests in God, it will gradually disappear unless he who retains it in perfect firmness intercedes as Mediator. Otherwise, God's majesty is too lofty to be attained by mortal men, who are like grubs crawling upon the earth" (II:VI:4).

Since Calvin believed that God brought salvation to those in the Old Testament who believed in Christ without knowing His name, do you think he would believe that people today who have never heard the name *Jesus* could believe in Christ without knowing His name? If yes, how do you think this might impact his (and your) motivation to bring the gospel to those who have never heard?

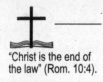

"Christ is the end of the law" (Rom. 10:4).

Emptying

"They are not fit to receive Christ's grace unless they first be emptied" (II:VII:11).

of David as a sort of "double mirror" in which Christ can be seen.

It is clear that the Law points beyond itself, Calvin said, because no one has ever been able to keep the whole Law. Rather, the guilt induced by the Law serves to arouse people to hope and to seek pardon from God, while at the same time rendering them inexcusable before God.

Calvin identified three functions of the law: (1) To free us from the delusion of our own goodness, from the "presumption of ficticious righteousness," and thereby to arouse us to seek God's grace. (2) To restrain the lusts and wickedness of the unregenerate, thereby protecting the human community from their unbridled evil. (3) And principally to guide believers toward the goal of perfect obedience to God.

Calvin distinguished between the power of the Law that is still in force for believers and the power of the Law that has been done away with. Although the Law still has power to exhort believers in godliness, the Law, he explained, is no longer an instrument of condemnation for believers, and the ceremonies of the Law are mere shadows, "in indistinct outline only" of what was completed in the work of Christ.

 COMMENTARY

This chapter contains its fair share of Calvin's colorful language, providing a variety of images that compress a complex doctrine into a few words. For example, Calvin, echoing Paul's words, described the Law as a "tutor unto Christ." Calvin pictured the Law as something helpful yet provisional. When Calvin spoke of "the prison house of the body," he painted a clear word picture of human life on earth, a life that is perpetually in bondage to the limitations of the flesh. And when he explained how the Law functions "to pinch them awake to their imperfection," Calvin vividly pictured the power of the Law to arouse believers from the drowsiness of sin, an image he established in Book 1.

A passing comment in this chapter may help those who find Calvin's teachings on providence and predestination overly harsh. "The reprobate" said Calvin, "always freely desire to evade God's judgment" (II:VII:9). There is evidence enough throughout the *Institutes* to make clear Calvin's understanding that all who remain in hell, in eternal separation from God, willfully choose to be there.

On Calvin's view, what are the three functions of the Law?

SUMMARY VIII: EXPLANATION OF THE TEN COMMANDMENTS

Calvin explained that God has given the written Law in order to awaken humans, blinded and sluggish as they are, to a knowledge of God that goes beyond the obscurity of the law of nature and the conscience alone. Calvin affirmed the good intent of the Law's severity, namely that it results in humility and self-abasement which leads us to flee to the mercy of God. God includes promises of rewards and threats of punishment in the Law, said Calvin, in order to arouse His people to a love for good and a hatred of evil. And He denounces the foolishness of seeking to please God apart from obeying God's Law.

Calvin explained that the Law must not simply be understood externally as a control for human behavior. Instead, the requirements of

Nothing More Acceptable to God

"Nothing is more acceptable to [God] than obedience. . . . In all ages this irreligious affectation of religion . . . has manifested itself . . . ; for men always delight in contriving some way of acquiring righteousness apart from God's Word" (II:VIII:5).

the Law extend beyond behavior to secret thoughts and motives, requiring an inward righteousness. Resisting the literalism of the Pharisees who congratulated themselves on the external avoidance of vice, Christ restored the Law of Moses to its original integrity by teaching the essence beneath the external requirements of the Commandments.

Calvin identified the two tables of the Ten Commandments, the first applying to the worship of God and the second to proper duties of humans to one another. After assigning the first four Commandments to the first table and the last six to the second table, Calvin began his explanation of the meaning of each of the Commandments:

The Preface—Calvin suggested that the beginning of the Commandments ("I am the Lord") should properly be understood as a preface which declares God's rightful claim on His people and God's unique identity as the deliverer of His people from bondage.

The First Commandment—Calvin explained that the prohibition against the worship of false gods contains the requirement that our worship of God ("true religion") must come first, "as the only goal of all the activities of this life."

The Second Commandment—The prohibition against graven images, Calvin explained, reveals the kind of spiritual worship God prescribes, one void of any attempt to create visible forms for God. Calvin went on to explain the purpose of God's threatening words following this Commandment ("who visits the iniquity of the fathers upon the children" (cp. Ezek. 18:20; Num. 14:18; Exod. 34:6–7; Jer. 32:18). He clarified that God does not punish the children for their parents' sins; rather, they are punished for their own sins, which they willfully and naturally choose, in imitation of their fathers. Calvin was careful to contrast the vastness of God's generosity with the limitation of His vengeance, pointing out that while God's punishment is limited to the fourth generation, God's mercy extends to a thousand generations.

The Third Commandment—The intent of this Commandment, said Calvin, is to declare that any speaking of God be done with reverence and soberness, not with flippancy or out of "ambition, or greed, or amusement." Calvin clarified what kinds of oaths are condemned by this Commandment: swearing by a false god, swearing by God's name and lying, and swearing true but trivial oaths in God's name. Calvin argued (against the Anabaptists) that Jesus' words about the giving of oaths were not meant to prohibit the use of oaths commended in the Law, teaching that oaths are allowable when they either "vindicate the Lord's glory" or "further a brother's edification."

The Fourth Commandment—Calvin offered three reasons for the Sabbath Commandment: (1) For believers to set aside their work in order to allow God to work in them; (2) for believers to assemble for training in piety; (3) for servants and those who work under human authority to have a day of rest from toil. Calvin suggested that the Sabbath Commandment points to the perfect rest God has promised His children, a rest that will not be fully entered into this side of heaven. Calvin taught that since Christ's coming abolished the ceremonial observance of this Commandment, its reach can no longer be limited to a single day but extends to the whole of life. Resisting the "superstitious observance of days" as a "shadow rite" (see Gal. 4:10–11),

Calvin nevertheless enjoined believers to observe sacred meetings frequently for the purpose of maintaining order among God's people in the church.

The Fifth Commandment—Calvin taught that the command to honor parents extends also to all those in authority over us, whether they are deserving or undeserving of that honor. Acknowledging that the keeping of this Commandment should be a step toward honoring God, Calvin taught that parents are not to be obeyed when they lead their children away from a true obedience to the Father.

The Sixth Commandment—The prohibition against killing, Calvin taught, extends to God's requirement that we exercise zeal in the care of our neighbors, both for their physical safety and for the "safety of the soul."

Living Together

"Outside marriage man cannot cohabit with a woman without God's curse" (II:VIII:41).

The Seventh Commandment—Far from being a mere prohibition against adultery, Calvin saw this Commandment as God's affirmative injunction to purity and modesty for all believers. Except for those blessed with the special grace of celibacy, Calvin admitted, most believers should turn to marriage as the "sole remedy" for escaping the temptation of unchastity.

The Eighth Commandment—Calvin extended the prohibition against stealing to include God's command to care for others' good, rendering to each person what is due according to his or her station in life.

The Ninth Commandment—Calvin extended the prohibition against bearing false witness to apply to the injunction for believers always to speak well of their neighbors, to avoid bitter taunts under the guise of joking, and not to listen to evil words about others.

The Tenth Commandment—The command against covetousness, according to Calvin, reminds believers that they are to banish from their minds everything that does not lead toward love of their neighbors.

Calvin summarized that the purpose of the Law is to conform believers to the "archetype of divine purity," that they might cleave to God. Calvin vehemently rejected two scholastic notions: (1) that some of Jesus' commandments are too difficult and should be seen as "counsels" and not commands, and (2) that sins should be divided between venial and mortal sins. Calvin affirmed that every sin is "deadly" and justly deserving of God's punishment.

COMMENTARY

Calvin spoke of "the law" in three different ways: (1) as the whole religion of Moses, (2) as the moral law which God gave by special revelation to His people, most uniquely seen in the Ten Commandments and in the Sermon on the Mount, and (3) as various bodies of ceremonial, civil, and judicial statutes. For Calvin the moral law is the most important.

Rejecting the notion that the Ten Commandments contain only the bare rudiments of faith, Calvin, like Jesus, extended the Commandments' reach beyond behavior to the realm of thoughts, motives, and "innermost righteousness," seen only by God. Obedience in our duties toward one another, therefore, is deeply dependent on the foundation of love and reverence for God. Contrary to those modern

Literal Interpretation?

"He who would confine his understanding of the law within the narrowness of the words deserves to be laughed at. . . . Now, I think this would be the best rule, . . . that is, in each commandment to ponder why it was given to us" (II:VIII:8).

Love of Self

"And obviously, since men were born in such a state that they are too much inclined to self-love, . . . there was no need of a law that would increase or rather enkindle this already excessive love. Hence it is very clear that we keep the commandments not by loving ourselves but by loving God and neighbor. . . . [God] does not concede the first place to self-love as certain Sophists stupidly imagine" (II:VIII:54).

In what ways does the Law apply to Christians?

teachers who suggest that we must love ourselves before we can properly love God or our neighbor, Calvin declared that humans know all too well how to love themselves.

Calvin's approach to the interpretation of the Law gives a helpful understanding of his approach to biblical interpretation, as he looked beyond external requirements in order to find God's underlying purpose for each Commandment. According to Calvin, the Ten Commandments condemn sin by categories, each Commandment a synecdoche, signifying the whole of God's requirement by mentioning the most "frightful and wicked element." In this way, the Commandments are able to condemn every sin without listing each individually.

Calvin's interpretation of the Sabbath Commandment reveals his underlying understanding of the importance of the believer's growing, daily relationship with Christ, refusing to limit this Commandment to an external observance of one holy day in seven. Calvin did not teach that the intent of the Sabbath was abolished in the work of Christ; rather, the scope of its influence was expanded to include our daily attentiveness to God, in which believers are called daily to make "fresh progress" toward a blessed rest in God.

SUMMARY IX: LAW AND GOSPEL

Calvin clarified that through the Law, the godly who came before Christ saw an indistinct shadow of what was to be revealed fully in Christ. But the difference between the Law and the gospel, said Calvin, is a difference not in meaning but in the clarity of the message. John the Baptist, Calvin explained, stood between the

Law and the gospel, raising the gospel to a more preeminent level.

He explained that those who have lived after Christ have the advantage of richly enjoying what those under the Law had only tasted. He acknowledged that even believers, though they have the benefit of seeing Christ "at midday," still, like the godly before Christ, wait in hopeful expectation for the full transformation that will be theirs after death.

Enjoying Christ

"We enjoy Christ only as we embrace Christ clad in his own promises" (II:IX:3).

 COMMENTARY

In this chapter, Calvin affirmed (almost parenthetically) that the godly who died before the coming of Christ are saved the same way as Christians, namely by believing in Christ. Calvin explained that they, too, are included in "the fellowship of the understanding and light that shine in the person of Christ."

What was Calvin's view of the destiny of human beings who lived before Christ?

SUMMARY X: SIMILARITY OF THE OLD AND NEW TESTAMENTS

In opposition to his opponent Servetus, Calvin affirmed that the patriarchs of the Old Testament participated in the same inheritance and hope for the same salvation as those who came after Christ.

Servetus

Michael Servetus's heretical teaching opposed the *Institutes* and questioned if God knew prior to the Fall that man would sin. In spite of his awareness of a warrant for his arrest, Servetus appeared in the congregation where Calvin was preaching and was promptly arrested and burned at the stake.

Calvin affirmed the unity between the Old and New Covenants, affirming that the two are actually one in the same, affirming again that those under the Old Covenant actually "knew Christ as Mediator." He argued that it is foolish to assume that God was primarily concerned about the material prosperity of the Israelites, seeing in the Old Testament promises, the expectation of a future life of spiritual abundance. He pointed out as well that the Old

The End of the Old Testament

"One cannot but say that the Old Testament always had its end in Christ and in eternal life" (II:X:4).

Covenant was based on God's grace and kindness alone, just like the New Covenant, denouncing the arrogance of Christians who see themselves as superior to Jews.

SUMMARY XI: DIFFERENCES BETWEEN THE TESTAMENTS

Calvin identified five ways the New Testament differs from the Old Testament:

1. The Old Testament represents spiritual benefits most often in terms of temporal benefits. The patriarchs saw in their earthly blessings, as in a mirror, the promise of their future inheritance. Relying on the imagery of Paul, Calvin described the Jewish nation as a "child heir," the church in its infancy.

2. The Old Testament foreshadowed and revealed Christ in images and ceremonies. The ceremonies, explained Calvin, were only accessories, appendages to the covenant fully revealed in Christ. And the Law was the child's tutor to lead the Jews to Christ.

3. The Old Testament is literal, while the New Testament is spiritual, the first written on stone tablets, the second on people's hearts. The Law, said Calvin, clarified what is right, but it did not give the power to change hearts to do what is right.

4. The Old Testament involved bondage; the new, freedom. Again relying on the imagery of Paul, Calvin portrayed those under the Old Covenant as the children of Hagar, children born by human works into bondage, and those under the New Covenant as the children of Sarah, those born by the promise into freedom.

5. The Old Testament referred to one nation; the new, to all nations. Calvin affirmed that God "lodged his covenant" in the "bosom" of the nation of Israel, eventually breaking down the wall that held the covenant within the boundaries of Israel.

After enumerating the differences between the testaments, Calvin asserted that no one should accuse God of being inconsistent and changeable, simply because God chose to relate to His people with different forms in different ages. To those who might question why God didn't relate to His world without figures and shadows from the very beginning, Calvin responded that we should not doubt that God has acted with justice and wisdom, even if God's reasons are hidden from us.

 ## COMMENTARY

As was true in the early church with the Marcionites, some in the church today give the Old Testament an insignificant, even trivial role for the Christian. Though clear about the differences between the two testaments, Calvin emphasized that both are God's revelation to His people. Calvin condemned the foolishness of those who see in the two testaments two completely different Gods.

As he described the differences between the testaments, he was careful to remind his readers that the foundation of both is the same, namely Christ. And he was clear that the saints of the Old Testament are to be numbered among those who have been "peculiarly chosen of God" and share in God's eternal blessing. Affirming that the saints under the Old Covenant have a

In Calvin's view, what
are the relationships
between the Old
Testament and the
New Testament?

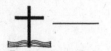

"For there is one God
and one mediator
between God and
men, the man Christ
Jesus" (1 Tim. 2:5).

sure hope of eternal life, Calvin explained that
the difference in the covenants is one of clarity:
What was given obscurely under the Law was
given with clarity in the gospel.

SUMMARY XII: THE NECESSITY OF CHRIST BECOMING HUMAN

Calvin explained that it was necessary for Christ
to become human because only one who was
both human and divine could serve as Mediator, bridging the gulf between God and humanity, a gulf so massive that even if humans were
without sin they would not be able to reach God
without a Mediator. According to Scripture,
Calvin said, there is no other reason given for
the coming of the Mediator than for the purpose
of paying the penalty for human sin and recon-
ciling humans to God. Calvin spent the remain-
der of the chapter giving his point-by-point
refutation of the "ignorant babblings" of Osiander who speculated that Christ would have
become flesh even if Adam had not sinned.

 COMMENTARY

Whenever the "why" questions are asked,
Calvin resorted to essentially the same answer:
because God, in His good and just wisdom,
secretly decreed it to be so. In response to his
contemporary opponent, Osiander, Calvin
argued that it is not right to ask unanswerable
questions of God, questions that are not clearly
dealt with in Scripture (for example, "Would
Christ have come if Adam had not sinned?" or
the more contemporary, frivolous question:
"Could God make a rock so large he couldn't
pick it up?")

What is Calvin's
attitude to questions
that are not clearly
answered in
Scripture?

SUMMARY XIII: CHRIST TRULY HUMAN

In the context of the ancient heretics, the Marcionites and the Manichees, each of whom denied the materiality of Christ's body, Calvin affirmed that Christ was truly human, characteristically basing his conclusion on an impressive collection of Scripture passages. He responded to those who would use entangling allegories to explain away the extensive scriptural evidence of Christ's humanity, and he saw in Christ, son of Adam, the "boundless grace" of God joining Himself to corrupt humanity.

 COMMENTARY

It was not only the ancient heretics that Calvin had in mind in this chapter but also Calvin's contemporary, Menno Simons, the founder of an Anabaptist group in the Netherlands, who denied that the Word truly united itself with human nature. (The Mennonites who came after him have not held to Menno's doctrine of the Incarnation.)

SUMMARY XIV: TWO NATURES IN ONE PERSON

Calvin affirmed the historic Christological doctrine, namely that the human and divine natures were joined together in the one person of Christ in a "hypostatic union." In his refutation of ancient heresies, he denounced both Nestorius who so pulled apart the natures of Christ as to devise a "double Christ" and Eutyches who so combined Christ's two natures that they were extinguished. Calvin clarified that though these two natures are joined together they are not fused into one nature. And though each of these two natures is unique, they are not separated from each other.

Something Marvelous

"Here is something marvelous: the Son of God descended from heaven in such a way that, without leaving heaven, he willed to be borne in the virgin's womb, to go about the earth, and to hang upon the cross; yet he continuously filled the world even as he had done from the beginning!" (II:XIII:4).

What was Calvin's view of the humanity of Jesus?

Two and One

"He who was the Son of God became the Son of man—not by confusion of substance, but by unity of person. For we affirm his divinity so joined and united with his humanity that each retains its distinctive nature unimpaired, and yet these two natures constitute one Christ" (II:XIV:1).

That Foul Dog

"Sane readers will gather from this summary that the crafty evasions of this foul dog [Servetus] utterly extinguish any hope of salvation" (II:XIV:8).

State succinctly Nestorius's and Eutyches's views of the two nature of Christ. How does Calvin differ from each?

Calvin condemned the errors of Michael Servetus, his contemporary opponent who taught that Christ only existed after He had been united to flesh. Calvin argued that Christ existed with God from the beginning and is, therefore, referred to as the "firstborn" of all creation. Though Calvin agreed that it might be useful for him to spend more time refuting the "grosser deceptions" of Servetus, he explained that since he had written an entire book exposing Servetus it would be superfluous to repeat those arguments here.

 COMMENTARY

In this chapter, Calvin's lawyer-like style of pressing his arguments is clearly seen. It was not uncommon for him to begin an argument by confidently summarizing its expected impact. He wrote, for example, "A little later I shall append some testimonies that will more effectively shatter that figment of theirs," and, "This observation will be highly useful in solving very many difficulties, if my readers apply it intelligently." When he was certain that he had found an enemy of the true faith, Calvin was not above name calling, throughout the *Institutes* referring to his opponents as "dogs" and to their arguments as "barkings" or "yelps."

SUMMARY XV: PROPHET, KING, AND PRIEST

Calvin identified that the title "*Christ*" refers to three specific offices: prophet, king, and priest, all of which receive the office by means of anointing. He explained that Christ's prophetic office means an end to all other prophecies, that nothing now needs to be added.

Calvin began his discussion of the kingly office by declaring that Christ is the fulfillment of God's promise of an eternal reign given to David. Calvin affirmed, therefore, that the church can never be overthrown. He explained that, by the power of the Holy Spirit, believers are armed and equipped by Christ the King for the struggle of this world. Christ's kingdom, Calvin was quick to point out, "does not consist in outward advantages" or "in earthly pleasures or pomp." Rather, our happiness is to be found in the heavenly life to come.

Christ's priestly office is seen in His perfect work as Mediator, standing between God and humanity. Here Calvin condemned the Roman doctrine of sacrificing Christ anew at each mass.

Unconquerable

"No matter how many strong enemies plot to overthrow the church, they do not have sufficient strength to prevail over God's immutable decree by which he appointed his Son eternal King. Hence it follows that the devil, with all the resources in the world, can never destroy the church" (II:XV:3).

 COMMENTARY

In this chapter, Calvin's view of the Roman church becomes clear as he referred to its adherents as the "papists," a term he used to describe them throughout the *Institutes*. Accusing them of misrepresenting Christ, Calvin asserted that though they may speak of Christ's threefold office they use these titles "coldly" and "ineffectively."

Against those present-day alarmists who teach that the church is just one generation from extinction, Calvin's doctrine of Christ's kingship declared that the future of the church does not depend on human efforts but on the reign of Christ. It is as believers grasp that they are as subjects of Christ's unassailable, invisible kingdom that they have courage to stand against adversaries that appear impossible to defeat.

What would Calvin say to those who wring their hands and say that the church is only one generation away from extinction?

SUMMARY XVI: CHRIST THE REDEEMER, PARTICULARLY IN THE APOSTLE'S CREED

Calvin affirmed that the only hope for "condemned, dead and lost" humanity is found in the redeeming work of Christ. All people, Calvin explained, if they take a serious look at who they are, see God's wrath and hostility toward them. But this inner awareness of God's wrath only serves to lead believers to an ardent awareness of God's benevolence toward them in Christ, since God's love for them began before the world was created.

Supported by the structure of the Apostles' Creed, Calvin affirmed that the redemptive work of Christ began when He took on human flesh and was completed at Christ's Ascension. In His condemnation by Pilate, said Calvin, Christ took the role of a guilty person, thereby dying in the place of the sinner. In His Crucifixion, Christ took the place of those under the curse, taking the burden of sin upon Himself. In His death and burial, He defeated the power of death and killed "the old man in us."

Calvin offered an extensive discussion of the credal phrase, "he descended into hell," admitting that this phrase has not enjoyed universal acceptance in the church, in spite of the fact that every one of the early fathers wrote of this doctrine. Calvin contended that it contains a most important mystery, by expressing the "hand to hand" combat which Christ endured in defeating the powers of hell and death. Calvin asserted that the creed rightly shows not only what Christ suffered in the sight of those on earth ("was crucified, dead and buried") but also what He suffered in the sight of God ("descended into hell"), enduring God's wrath

God Finds Something to Love

"All of us surely displease God, are guilty in his sight, and are born to the damnation of hell. But because the Lord wills not to lose what is his in us, out of his own kindness he still finds something to love" (II:XVI:3).

toward the wicked. According to Calvin, all of Christ's suffering in the garden and His cries from the cross were not a mere struggle with the dread of common death but with the punishment His soul would endure.

Calvin explained that although Christ's death satisfies the requirements of God's just judgment against us, we are reborn not through Christ's death alone but through His Resurrection. Calvin so linked Christ's death and Resurrection that whenever one is spoken of, the other should be assumed.

Calvin explained that although Christ's Ascension meant the end of His physical presence, it made way for His spiritual presence to come. His place "at the right hand of the Father" assures believers that their way to heaven has now been opened, that the throne which would have been filled with dread is now filled with grace and kindness. And Calvin affirmed the certainty of Christ's coming judgment, declaring the good news that our Judge is now none other than our Redeemer.

COMMENTARY

The heart of Calvin's message in this chapter is the centrality of Christ. To know the heart of the Christian faith, for Calvin, is to know Christ, the only hope of salvation.

Some suggest that Christ's descent into hell was for the purpose of His preaching to those souls who had already died, as if the patriarchs who had hoped in the coming Christ were condemned to a sort of "Limbo" until the coming of Christ. Calvin referred to this idea as a childish story without evidence in Scripture. As he

Death and Resurrection

"Through his death, sin was wiped out and death extinguished; through his resurrection, righteousness was restored and life raised up, so that—thanks to the resurrection—his death manifested its power and efficacy in us" (II:XVI:13).

Christ Alone

"If, then, we would be assured that God is pleased with and kindly disposed toward us, we must fix our eyes . . . on Christ alone" (II:XVI:3). "We see that our whole salvation and all its parts are comprehended in Christ. We should therefore take care not to derive the least portion of it from anywhere else" (II:XVI:19).

affirmed earlier, Calvin taught here that the godly before Christ who looked to Him for salvation (even before He was born) gained entrance into heaven as surely as do those who after Christ put their trust in Him.

Calvin modeled his third form of Christian freedom (the freedom to be indifferent about indifferent things) when he wrote about the authorship of the Apostles' Creed. Here, he was not afraid of scholarship that might suggest that the creed bearing the apostle's name might not have been written by their hands. He held to the central concern by acknowledging that, regardless of who wrote the creed, it proclaims accurately and in the right order a biblically based summary of the Christian faith. Though he did not shy away from theological conflict, Calvin refused to engage in debate about "pointless" quarrels like this one, denouncing those who are unwilling to hear a truth given by the Holy Spirit simply because they cannot say with certainty through which human instrument God chose to speak.

SUMMARY XVII: CHRIST'S MERIT, OUR SALVATION

Calvin resisted any attempt to set Christ's merit against God's mercy. Rather he emphasized that Christ's merit is an expression of God's mercy, the true first cause of our salvation. Calvin appealed repeatedly to Scripture to show the substitutionary work of Christ, taking the curse of sinners upon Himself, paying the ransom price to redeem fallen humanity.

After reading Book 2, chapter 16, contrast Calvin's view of the phrase, "He descended into hades," with those of some earlier theologians.

Salvation by What Cause?

"We see how God's love holds first place, as the highest cause or origin; how faith in Christ follows this as the second or proximate cause" (II:XVII:2).

COMMENTARY

Calvin intentionally concluded Book 2 by affirming the preeminent role of God's love and mercy. Apparently aware of the potential contradiction of affirming that God loved us and was angry toward us at the same time, Calvin found the resolution to this paradox not in any rational explanation but simply in the inscrutable character of God. Again, Calvin allowed his theological curiosity to be bridled by his reverence for God and his tacit admission that much about God's ways is incomprehensible to an instrument as feeble as the human mind.

How?

"For, in some ineffable way, God loved us and yet was angry toward us at the same time, until he became reconciled to us in Christ" (II:XVII:2).

If someone asked you how God can love us and be angry at us at the same time, what explanation would you offer?

BOOK THREE: THE MEANS, THE BENEFITS, AND THE EFFECTS OF GRACE

"It now remains to pour into the heart itself what the mind has absorbed. For the Word of God is not received by faith if it flits about in the top of the brain, but when it takes root in the depth of the heart" (III:II:36).

Following the outline of the Apostles' Creed, Calvin dealt with the knowledge of God the Father in Book 1 and of God the Son in Book 2. In Book 3, he moved to his treatment of the Holy Spirit. Under this broad topic, Calvin discussed the work of the Holy Spirit in repentance, faith, and justification, as well as the nature of the Christian life. And before concluding the book with a discussion of life after death, Calvin explained his doctrine of election.

BOOK-AT-A-GLANCE

I   The Secret Work of the Spirit
II The Definition of Faith
III–V   The Doctrine of Repentance
VI–VII The Christian Life of Self-Denial
VIII–X The Future Life and the Present Life
XI–XIX The Doctrine of Justification

SUMMARY I: THE SECRET WORK OF THE SPIRIT

In answer to the understood question at the beginning of Book 3—How do we receive the grace and benefits of Christ?—Calvin's answer is clear: through the Holy Spirit. Calvin explained that the Holy Spirit is the bond that unites us to Christ and that faith is the Spirit's principle work. After describing the many names used for the Holy Spirit in the Scripture, Calvin referred to the Spirit as the "key that unlocks for us the treasures of the Kingdom of Heaven," affirming that any teaching about the true God is in vain unless the "inner Schoolmaster" teaches and draws believers to the Father.

"Until our minds become intent upon the Spirit, Christ, so to speak, lies idle because we coldly contemplate him as outside ourselves—indeed, far from us" (III:I:3).

What, in Calvin's view, are some of the roles of the Holy Spirit in the Christian's life?

 COMMENTARY

Consistent with his earlier teachings, Calvin had little interest in a cold, speculative understanding of God at a distance. The heart of Calvin's message is not simply about God but about what God has to do with us. Using perhaps the most intimate image available, Calvin pictured the Spirit's work as bringing believers into "sacred wedlock" with God.

SUMMARY II: THE DEFINITION OF FAITH

Calvin began his definition of faith by contrasting it with the Scholastic notion of "implicit faith," rejecting the idea that faith is the "cold" assent to a set of ideas or a mere passive acceptance of the church's teachings. He willingly admitted that true faith is always surrounded by clouds of errors due to the limitations of the human condition, recognizing that unbelief and faith are always mixed together. But, he argued, there is a radical distinction between those who, striving earnestly to learn more of God, admit their unbelief and those who "sluggishly rest" in their ignorance.

Calvin described the indivisible bond that exists between faith and God's Word, much like the relationship between the sun and its rays. He explained that we are drawn to faith by the promise of God's grace and mercy, revealed through the gospel.

Though Calvin admitted that there are a variety of uses for the word *faith* in the Scriptures, his primary concern was to clarify the meaning of that sort of faith by which believers "cross over from death into life." He emphasized that this faith consists of an assurance more than a comprehension, an assurance that is instructed more by God's truth than by any rational proofs.

Our oneness with Christ, said Calvin, gives an "indestructible certainty" to our faith. While recognizing that God cannot be comprehended by our inadequate human capacities, Calvin nevertheless affirmed that unbelief "does not hold sway within believers' hearts." He admitted that the faith of every believer is tinged with doubt—that though every believer holds a certain foundational assurance, that assurance is often assailed with doubt. Acknowledging this condition as a normal condition of faith, he urged believers to make continuous, steady progress toward a surer knowledge of God.

Faith Defined

"Now we shall possess a right definition of faith if we call it a firm and certain knowledge of God's benevolence toward us, founded upon the truth of the freely given promise in Christ, both revealed to our minds and sealed upon our hearts through the Holy Spirit" (III:II:7).

Personal Faith

"Here, indeed, is the chief hinge on which faith turns: that we do not regard the promises of mercy that God offers as true only outside ourselves, but not at all in us; rather that we make them ours by inwardly embracing them" (III:II:16).

Division in the Godly Heart

"Therefore the godly heart feels in itself a division because it is partly imbued with sweetness . . . ; partly grieves in bitterness . . . ; partly rests upon the promise of the gospel, partly trembles at the evidence of its own iniquity; partly rejoices at the expectation of life, partly shudders at death. This variation arises from imperfection of faith, since in the course of the present life it never goes so well with us that we are wholly cured of the disease of unbelief and entirely filled and possessed by faith" (III:II:18).

Faith, Word, and Spirit

"But our mind has such an inclination to vanity that it can never cleave fast to the truth of God; and it has such a dullness that it is always blind to the light of God's truth. Accordingly, without the illumination of the Holy Spirit, the Word can do nothing" (III:II:33).

Calvin distinguished between the fear of God that prods believers to restrain their presumption and shake off their sluggishness and the kind of fear that leads to despair, unable to rest in God's mercy. He suggested that it is possible—even helpful—for believers to possess the first kind of fear and still rest in the surest consolation of God's mercy.

Affirming that God is not simply the author of our faith but also its "eternal guardian," Calvin explained that the foundation of faith is the freely given promise of grace in Christ. But this promise cannot be grasped, said Calvin, apart from the Word of God, and the Word cannot be embraced apart from the illuminating work of the Holy Spirit, who not only initiates faith but sustains it as well. Though we are by nature blinded by God's splendor, the Spirit's illumination, explained Calvin, gives us the ability to see and to contemplate the splendor which had previously blinded us.

Calvin repeatedly emphasized that faith cannot be destroyed by doubt since our confidence rests not in the insecure foundation of our own works but in the freely given promise of God. Calvin rejected the notion that the assurance of our salvation is in suspense until our final day, arguing that the Holy Spirit seals the promises of God in our hearts with certainty.

Calvin declared that faith produces love for God in us, arousing us to enjoy the fullness of God once we have tasted the "abundant sweetness" which God has for us. In a similar way, Calvin linked faith and hope, faith being the foundation of hope and hope invigorating faith with the sure and certain expectation of the full manifestation of God's promises.

COMMENTARY

Again, Calvin would not allow his readers to be satisfied with passively accepting information about God (even an accurate knowledge of God). In his arguments against the Scholastics ("the Schoolmen"), he pushed his readers to understand that unless their knowledge of God moves them beyond mental assent to a certainty of heart before God, such knowledge cannot properly be called faith. Many today (even among those who claim to follow Calvin) so emphasize Calvin's thinking that they completely miss his emphasis on the necessity of "piety," what modern Christians might refer to as a personal experience of God. For Calvin, unless faith is a matter of the heart, it cannot be considered true faith at all.

Calvin clarified that illusory faith is found among those who are not elect. The key distinction between this faith and the true faith is that though the wicked may for a time be touched by divine grace their faith does not persevere but remains only for a time. In this context, Calvin affirmed again the doctrine of election, attempting to explain the predestination of the wicked to their deserved judgment.

Even as he talked about faith, Calvin repeated his common refrain: the utter faithfulness and power of God and the complete impotence of the human condition. For Calvin, all true knowledge of God is linked to an accurate knowledge of one's own condition.

Calvin explained, as well, that faith does not assure us of comfort or riches in this life. Rather, the chief expectation of faith, according

Think!

"Is this what believing means—to understand nothing, provided only that you submit your feeling obediently to the church? Faith rests not on ignorance, but on knowledge.... It is not enough for a man implicitly to believe what he does not understand or even investigate" (III:II:2). "For faith consists in the knowledge of God in Christ, not in reverence for the church" (III:II:3).

Faith in the Reprobate?

"For though only those predestined to salvation receive the light of faith and truly feel the power of the gospel, yet experience shows that the reprobate are sometimes affected by almost the same feeling as the elect, so that even in their own judgment they do not in any way differ from the elect ... but because the Lord, to render them more convicted and inexcusable, steals into their minds to the extent that his goodness may be tasted without the Spirit of adoption" (III:II:11).

Distrusting Ourselves

"For nothing so moves us to repose our assurance and certainty of mind in the Lord as distrust of ourselves, and the anxiety occasioned by the awareness of our ruin" (III:II:22).

What is Calvin's view regarding the assurance of salvation—even in this life?

to Calvin, is in the life to come, the hope of eternal salvation being the "inseparable companion" of faith.

SUMMARY III: REPENTANCE

In this chapter, Calvin sought to move from doctrine to description, affirming that his doctrine of regeneration would be obscure if he did not add an "explanation of the effects we feel." Though repentance and faith are, for Calvin, held together by "permanent bond," he insisted that repentance is a *result* of faith, not its cause. And he denounced those who view repentance as a short-term, preconversion experience rather than a lifelong practice for believers.

Relying on the vocabulary of the ancient fathers, Calvin affirmed that true repentance consists of two parts: mortification of the flesh (the putting to death of the old self) and vivification of the Spirit (the receiving of new life in Christ). Distinguishing between the repentance of the Law and the repentance of the gospel, he explained that those who experience the former kind (Judas, for example) are stung with the gravity of their sin but without the hope of forgiveness, while the latter not only admit their sin but also trust in God's goodness to forgive.

Calvin affirmed that, though believers move forward toward sanctification through repentance, they are never able to achieve a sinless perfection in this life. Even those who are regenerate, he explained, possess a "smoldering cinder of evil" as long as they live. And although sin no longer reigns in the life of the believer, the presence of sin remains; and so, according to Calvin, believers are free from the guilt of sin but not from the desire to sin. Appealing to Romans 6 (see v. 12), Calvin noted that Paul did not say,

"Let sin not be," but, "Let sin not reign," obviously assuming that the presence of sin would still remain in the believer.

Calvin joined repentance and forgiveness of sins, affirming that the entire gospel can be understood under these two headings. He reaffirmed that it is not human repentance that moves God to forgive; rather it is the mercy and promise of God's forgiveness that leads believers to repent. We learn to hate sin, in other words, only after we have first learned to love righteousness.

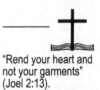

"Rend your heart and not your garments" (Joel 2:13).

Calvin resisted any attempt to link true repentance to mere external practices of penance, though he did not reject the practice of fasting and weeping in repentance. He offered his explanation of the unpardonable sin, explaining that this sin cannot be committed accidentally or in ignorance but occurs only in those who have been convinced of the genuineness of the Word of God and repudiate it anyway. He made clear that the unforgivable sin is not a matter of a single lapse in judgment but rather a "universal rebellion," "a complete turning away," in which the reprobate repeatedly rejects that offer of salvation.

The Source of Regeneration

"Yet the efficacy of this depends upon the Spirit of regeneration. For it would be easier for us to create men than for us of our own power to put on a more excellent nature" (III:III:21).

 COMMENTARY

Calvin made an important distinction in the order of faith and repentance. While many today might teach that salvation comes as a result of repentance, Calvin taught that faith comes before repentance. Consistent with his overriding concern throughout the *Institutes* that the initiative in our salvation belongs to

Daily Growth

"And indeed, this restoration does not take place in one moment or one day or one year; but through continual and sometimes even slow advances God wipes out in his elect the corruptions of the flesh, cleanses them of guilt, consecrates them to himself as temples renewing all their minds to true purity that they may practice repentance all their lives and know that this warfare will end only at death" (III:III:9).

Prevenient Grace

"It is certain that the mind of man is not changed for the better except by God's prevenient grace. Also, his promise to those who call upon him will never deceive. But it is improper to designate as 'conversion' and 'prayer' the blind torment that distracts the reprobate when they see that they must seek God in order to find a remedy for their misfortunes and yet flee at his approach" (III:III:24).

God, Calvin insisted that no one can truly repent without first having faith.

Like a pastor concerned that his flock not become discouraged by their own failings, Calvin affirmed that repentance is a lifetime process of regeneration. Again in this context, he affirmed that it is the daily practice of repentance that moves believers more toward the restoration of the image of God that was nearly obliterated in Adam's Fall. For Calvin, this restoration is not a once-and-for-all, instantaneous event, but it is often a slow and incremental process.

Calvin also distinguished between the false repentance of the reprobate and the true repentance of the regenerate. The first may turn to God in prayer, but they later flee from Him. The latter turn to God, not only "rending their garments" but their hearts as well.

SUMMARY IV–V: SCHOLASTIC DOCTRINES OF REPENTANCE REFUTED

In these chapters, Calvin clarified his own doctrine of repentance by refuting the doctrine of one of his primary theological opponents, the Scholastics. He denounced the Scholastic emphasis on external ceremonies of repentance, practices that deal little with the inward change that true repentance requires. Calvin explained that the Scholastic's teaching can naturally lead believers to assume that their only hope of forgiveness rests in their own contrition. And since the doctrine of penance depends so heavily on human works, Calvin explained, it can never lead believers to an assurance of their own forgiveness, leaving their consciences perpetually tormented by uncertainty.

With his characteristic dependence on the precedents of church history, Calvin explained that, in the ancient church, compulsory confession was not an established practice. He then turned to the Scripture to establish the "simple," biblical requirements for the confession of sins.

Contrary to the Roman practice of "confession," the relating of one's sins to the priests, Calvin urged a mutual confession in which believers frequently admit their sinfulness to one another. Although recognizing the freedom of Christians to confess their sins to whomever they consider most suitable, he acknowledged that pastors are especially entrusted with the duty of hearing private confession "in the cure of souls." He affirmed the need for the worshiping community to confess their sins corporately, and he urged pastors to form prayers of confession for their churches on every Lord's Day.

"Therefore confess your sins to each other and pray for each other so that you may be healed" (Jas. 5:16).

In contrast to the Roman doctrine that identifies the "power of the keys" in the forgiveness spoken by the priest, Calvin insisted that the power of the keys rests in the preaching of the gospel and in the inherent power of God's Word, not in the priests. He utterly rejected the Roman requirement of complete confession, acknowledging that no person knows completely the full gravity of all their sins. For Calvin, the expectation of complete confession is a foolish impossibility, one which has the potential to bring about "measureless torment." Under this system, one cannot find any place to rest in the certainty of God's pardon in Christ.

"Who can discern his errors? Forgive my hidden faults" (Ps. 19:12).

A Sure Rule

"But a very sure rule for making confession was to recognize and confess that the abyss of our evil is beyond our comprehension" (III:IV:18).

Calvin explained that since Scripture never links the forgiveness of Christ to the secret confession of sins to a priest, the "Romanists" have no grounds for placing this rule upon believers. Calvin affirmed repeatedly that the Christian's assurance of absolution from sin does not come

"Aquinas, the father of the scholastic theologians, taught that sin cannot be taken away without the sacrament of penance" (*Summa Theologica*, III.lxxxvi.4).

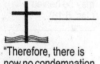

"Therefore, there is now no condemnation for those who are in Christ Jesus" (Rom. 8:1).

Who Gets Affliction?

"Since all of us, however, have such hardness and ignorance as to need chastisement, our most wise Father saw fit to exercise all of us without exception throughout life with a common scourge" (III:IV:35).

from the judgment of a "priestling" but from the assurance of pardon found in the freely given promises of God.

Calvin taught that the sacrifice of Christ is the "sole offering for sins, the sole expiation, the sole satisfaction." According to Calvin, any doctrine that makes the forgiveness offered in Christ dependent on some human work (even the "work" of penance) completely misunderstands God's grace, depriving the Christian conscience of assurance before God.

Calvin rejected the distinction between mortal and venial sins, as if some sins deserved the penalty of death and others did not. He explained that all sins are deserving of death and are, therefore, mortal. The sins of believers are venial, according to Calvin, not because they do not deserve death, but because by God's mercy they are forgiven.

Calvin distinguished between God's judgment in vengeance and God's judgment in chastisement. He explained that God treats the impious with justice, giving them over to the "penal sentence" of death; but God punishes believers like a father, chastising his children with "medicinal pain" for their good. Calvin affirmed that God gives different chastisement to different people as he deems expedient, and he urges believers to be fortified by this knowledge, trusting in every affliction that their loving Father is working in them for good.

In chapter 5, Calvin condemned the Roman practice of indulgences and their doctrine of purgatory, asserting that both indulgences and purgatory are absolutely contrary to the teachings of the Scripture. And he saw beneath both doctrines the false theological assumption that forgiveness of sins depends at least in part on human merit.

He vehemently rejected the unbiblical superstitions of purgatory and praying for the dead, claiming that many of the ancient writers shared a "common ignorance" in this regard.

COMMENTARY

Calvin's refutation of the scholastic doctrine of repentance is twice as long as his explanation of his own doctrine of repentance. Calvin, like most theologians, was able to give the most clarity to his own doctrines by contrasting them with those of his opponents. Having been educated as a young man in the medieval scholastic tradition in his own preparation for the priesthood, Calvin sought to clarify for his readers how the dominant theological assumptions of his culture are false. With the extensive reforms in the Roman Catholic Church since Vatican II, much of Calvin's vehement attack on the Catholic church may appear overstated for our time. But these chapters do, in addition to clarifying Calvin's own doctrine of repentance, present a clearer picture of the theological landscape against which his own ideas were formed.

In these chapters, Calvin showed again his pastoral concern that believers find a sure and certain place to rest in the forgiveness and grace of God. His vehement attacks on the Roman church in these chapters find their passion in his concern that believers are held in torment, anxiety, and fear because of the church's false doctrine of the forgiveness of sins. He refused to accept the bondage that reduces the forgiveness

A Deadly Fiction of Satan

"But when expiation of sins is sought elsewhere than in the blood of Christ, when satisfaction is transferred elsewhere, silence is very dangerous. Therefore, we must cry out with the shouting not only of our voices but of our throats and lungs that purgatory is a deadly fiction of Satan, which nullifies the cross of Christ, inflicts unbearable contempt upon God's mercy, and overturns and destroys our faith" (III:V:6).

On His Opponents

"They have involved this matter, otherwise not very complicated, in so many volumes that there would be no easy way out if you were to immerse yourself even slightly in their slime" (III:IV:1).
"I shall add certain other testimonies by which these wriggling snakes may be so held fast that after this they will be unable to coil up even the tip of their tail" (III:IV:29).
"These men are fit to be treated by drugs for insanity rather than to be argued with" (III:V:1).

of sins to the whim of a priest (or "priestling," the pejorative term Calvin was fond of using). Both to those held in perpetual fear about their own standing with God and to those who presume that an annual ceremonial confession assures them of pardon, Calvin's doctrine offers a comforting and a challenging corrective.

Chapter 4 gives Calvin's readers another sample of his approach to Scripture, as he urged his readers not to trust his commentary but simply to yield to the clear testimonies of God's Word. And Calvin treated the writings of the church fathers in the same way, holding their teaching up to the light of the Scriptures. For example, throughout the *Institutes*, Calvin relied heavily on the teachings of Augustine, finding in the African bishop's writings much support for his own views. But when it came to Augustine's reflections on praying for his dead mother, Calvin declared that this was a case in which Augustine did not test his doctrine by the norm of the Scripture.

Don't Trust Calvin

"Here I must adjure my readers not to heed my glosses, but only to yield some place to the Word of God" (III:IV:29).

Many modern Christians have enough knowledge of church history to recall that Luther, at the beginning of the Reformation, condemned the sale of indulgences for the forgiveness of sins. And today, almost every contemporary Christians would reject this practice. But, in many ways, this practice simply grew out of a theology that based forgiveness of sin on human merits and practices. Though it may be hard for modern Christians to understand why Calvin spent such voluminous energy clarifying why human works do not bring about forgiveness of sins, the truth is that his clear teaching about grace strikes at the root of theological aberrations like the practice of selling indulgences. The gradual growth of the practice of selling indulgences gives modern Christians a compelling case study of the far-reaching impact of theological assumptions.

SUMMARY VI: THE CHRISTIAN LIFE

Calvin identified two key components to the Christian life: (1) having the love of righteousness firmly established in our hearts, and (2) having a rule of righteousness set forth for us by God. Calvin contrasted the Christian motivation for virtue with that of the philosophers, who exhort their listeners to act virtuously simply because such action is in accordance with nature. Christians, on the other hand, have a clear pattern for life given by the Author of life itself, Christ being our example of perfect righteousness.

Calvin insisted that the Christian life is not primarily a matter of orthodox words or right action. Rather, he affirmed, it must begin in the inmost heart of the believer; only then can it be translated into right words and righteous living.

Calvin identified that the sum of the Christian life is to be found in self-denial.

COMMENTARY

Though Calvin was relentless in his affirmation of God's demand for holiness in believers' lives, still he acknowledged that absolute perfection in following God's commands is impossible. He encouraged his readers, therefore, to press on to make daily progress in righteousness, despite how slow and incremental such progress might seem.

In Calvin's view, is it possible to make a complete confession of one's sin? Explain.

Affections of the Heart

"For it is a doctrine not of the tongue but of life. It is not apprehended by the understanding and memory alone, as other disciplines are, but it is received only when it possesses the whole soul, and finds a seat and resting place in the inmost affection of the heart" (III:VI:4).

Christian Growth

"Let each one of us, then, proceed according to the measure of his puny capacity and set out upon the journey we have begun. . . . Therefore, let us not cease so to act that we may make some unceasing progress in the way of the Lord. And let us not despair at the slightness of our success" (III:VI:5).

Why did Calvin say that we should not be surprised at "the slightness of our success" as we grow in grace?

Forget about Ourselves

"We are not our own; in so far as we can, let us therefore forget ourselves and all that is ours. . . . Let this therefore be the first step, that a man depart from himself in order that he may apply the whole force of his ability in the service of the Lord" (III:VII:1).

"Therefore, I urge you, brothers, in view of God's mercy, to offer your bodies as living sacrifices, holy and pleasing to God" (Rom. 12:1).
"I no longer live, but Christ lives in me" (Gal. 2:20).

SUMMARY VII: SELF-DENIAL

Recognizing that each person is sinfully preoccupied with his or her own well-being, Calvin asserted that the heart of the Christian life requires believers to take the attention off themselves and willfully enlist themselves in service to God and humanity. Calvin was under no illusion that this is an easy process, admitting that humans, by their very nature, seek to minimize their own sins and congratulate themselves for their own virtues.

Calvin affirmed that the Christian life begins with the recognition that every aspect of the believer's life belongs to God. It is the sense of resignation to God's will, Calvin claimed, that frees believers to serve their neighbors with eagerness and genuine love. He urged believers not simply to go through the motions of serving others but to do so out of a "sincere feeling of love," looking not to the merit of the ones being served but to the image of God in them.

 COMMENTARY

Calvin began his entire discussion of the nature of the Christians' life by establishing the foundation of self-denial as the essential starting point, the "sum of the Christians life." Though "stewardship" in many churches is seen as nothing more than a spiritualized synonym for fund-raising, Calvin's notion of Christian stewardship was much deeper, insisting that God alone owns everything a Christian has, even the Christian's life itself. Only after a believer has fully grasped God's complete ownership of everything can he or she begin to understand the superficiality of a "stewardship" that focuses on a tithe that is given to God, while neglecting the requirement of self-denial with the other 90 percent.

SUMMARY VIII: THE EXPERIENCE OF BEARING THE CROSS

Calvin taught that bearing the cross (the Christian's experiencing pain and affliction) is a necessary and normal part of the Christian life. He identified a number of benefits Christians experience in bearing the cross: (1) It shows the feebleness of the human condition and our utter dependence on God. (2) It teaches us to trust God's faithfulness. (3) It trains us in us patience and obedience. (4) It restrains our flesh with the medicine of affliction. (5) It chastises the children of God and moves them to repentance. (6) The cross of persecution for righteousness sake serves as a "special badge of . . . soldiery." (7) It provides an opportunity for Christians to find their consolation in God.

How does Calvin's view of stewardship differ from that which is widely held?

Calvin went on to contrast the Christian approach to pain with that of the Stoics, affirming that Christians express their sorrow and pain, while the Stoics see virtue in responding to adversity "like a stone," considering weeping or groaning in sadness to be a sin. For Calvin, the Christian life is not about the denial of emotions but about resigning ourselves to the providence of God, especially in times of pain and affliction. Calvin concluded this chapter by affirming that Christian suffering is always tempered with a sense of spiritual joy.

 COMMENTARY

While affirming that there is immense comfort and assurance to be found at the base of the Christian life, Calvin also made clear that the

Hard Life

"Whomever the Lord has adopted and deemed worthy of his fellowship ought to prepare themselves for a hard, toilsome, and unquiet life, crammed with very many and various kinds of evil. It is the Heavenly Father's will thus to exercise them so as to put his own children to a definite test" (III:VIII:1).

What benefits does crossbearing bring to us?

No Progress Without It

"Let us, however, consider this settled: that no one has made progress in the school of Christ who does not joyfully await the day of death and final resurrection" (III:IX:5).

Christian life is inherently one of affliction, pain, and toil. Most Christians would agree on this point, but Calvin's more controversial assertion in this chapter is that God is the Author of every affliction. Many would resist Calvin's conclusion here, assuming that such a doctrine makes God into a capricious monster rather than a loving Father. But Calvin's primary aim, it seems, is not to induce fear but comfort, urging believers to rest in the knowledge that no affliction can touch them apart from God's powerful and protective care. Since suffering is a certainty for all humans, Calvin's doctrine is one that can not only prepare believers for the toil and pain of life but also encourage them with the knowledge that God is in control, no matter how chaotic their lives may be. In an age when Christians easily embrace a gospel of comfort, one that prepares believers to be surprised by pain, Calvin's teachings offer a helpful corrective.

SUMMARY IX: MEDITATION ON THE FUTURE LIFE

Calvin explained that God uses our tribulations to disengage from an excessive love of this world. He affirmed the vanity of this present life, acknowledging the foolish human tendency to seek happiness exclusively in this transient and unsatisfying world. Though Calvin taught that contempt for this present life is essential to the Christian life, he nevertheless affirmed that this life and all its benefits are to be received with gratitude from God's hand. Calvin taught that a joyful longing for the future life in God's presence should be normative for every Christian.

COMMENTARY

It is no accident that Calvin's discussion on the meditation on the future life immediately followed his discussion of the pain of bearing the cross. To his way of thinking, a clear expectation of our future in heaven is essential to a proper response to affliction and pain. He insisted that God uses affliction to remove our obsessive attempts at gaining happiness in this life and to draw our minds to the future life prepared for us.

SUMMARY X: THE PRESENT LIFE

Calvin established three rules for the proper use of good things: (1) Good things are to be enjoyed as gifts of God. (2) Believers should take care that good things not lead them to a lifestyle of indulgence. (3) Believers are given every good thing as a trust from God for which they will be held accountable as stewards of God's resources. Calvin warned against an excessive concern about the things of this life to the exclusion of the concerns of the soul; and in this regard, he repeated his previous admonition that believers practice a contempt for this life and a meditation upon the life to come.

 COMMENTARY

Here, Calvin again touched on his doctrine of stewardship, affirming that all worldly goods that we receive are given to us as a trust from God. He took this idea a step further by urging believers to learn contentment with their station in life, avoiding excessive ambition and the resulting desire for more and more things.

If This World . . .

"For, if heaven is our homeland, what else is the earth but our place of exile? If departure from the world is entry into life, what else is the world but a sepulcher? . . . If to be freed from the body is to be released into perfect freedom, what else is the body but a prison?" (III:IX:4).

"I know what it is to be in need, and I know what it is to have plenty. I have learned the secret of being content in any and every situation, whether well fed or hungry, whether living in plenty or in want" (Phil. 4:12).

What values does Calvin see in our contemplating the life to come?

SUMMARY XI: JUSTIFICATION BY FAITH DEFINED

Calvin affirmed that justification is the "main hinge" on which our faith turns. He therefore offered an extensive discussion on the meaning of justification, beginning by defining three related terms:

1. When the Bible speaks of a person being *justified in God's sight*, it refers to that person no longer being reckoned a sinner before God but being reckoned as righteous.
2. *Justification by works* refers to the process by which a person might stand before God's judgment with such purity and holiness that he or she deserves to be accounted righteous before God.
3. *Justification by faith* occurs when a believer does not trust his or her own righteousness but embraces the righteousness of Christ by faith, receives forgiveness of sins, and is reckoned righteous before God.

Calvin left no place for works in his definition of *justification by faith*, declaring that the righteousness of Christ is imputed to believers, not making them forever free from sin but reckoning them as righteous in God's sight. Calvin asserted that believers cannot be justified by both faith and works, since even a particle of works for righteousness gives cause for boasting.

Much of this chapter centers around Calvin's refutation of Osiander, who taught that believers are "infused" with genuine righteousness at justification, not merely imputed righteousness. Calvin vehemently resisted this notion, affirming that justified believers remain sinners even after their justification.

The Vessel of Faith

"We compare faith to a kind of vessel; for unless we come empty and with the mouth of our soul open to seek Christ's grace, we are not capable of receiving Christ. . . . Faith, even though of itself it is of no worth or price, can justify us by bringing Christ, just as a pot crammed with money makes a man rich" (III:XI:7).

Osiander

Andreas Osiander, a Lutheran theologian and contemporary of Calvin, died less than ten years before the publication of the final edition of the *Institutes*. Osiander's doctrine of justification so emphasized the indwelling of the divine Christ that he dramatically minimized the justifying results of the human death of Christ.

In his discussions on justification, Calvin also broadened the commonly held notion of sin. For Calvin, sin was not simply an infraction against a moral code. Rather, it is "division between man and God" that is at the root of the human condition, and it is this division that is removed at justification through the forgiveness of sins.

"But your iniquities have separated you from your God; your sins have hidden his face from you, so that he will not hear" (Isa. 59:2).

COMMENTARY

Again in this chapter Calvin returned to his customary tactic of clarifying his own doctrine by contrasting it with that of an opponent. Reaffirming much that he had written earlier, he resisted any doctrine that in any way mingles the free gift of justification in Christ with the earned merit of human works, declaring that our righteousness is not in us but in Christ.

"Not having a righteousness of my own that comes from the law, but that which is through faith in Christ—the righteousness that comes from God and is by faith" (Phil. 3:9).

Consistent with his message throughout the *Institutes*, Calvin here took pains to clarify that there is nothing about our justification that is not a gift. Neither our decision to embrace Christ, nor our purity of life after our justification, Calvin declared, find their source in our own goodness. Even our openness to receive the gift of forgiveness, Calvin would say is a gift of God's grace. By contrast, many Christians today might naturally find themselves on the side of Calvin's opponents in this matter, asserting the primacy of the human decision in salvation. Calvin would likely respond to modern believers who place such confidence in human decision that they have forgotten that their ability and even their desire to "decide" for God are themselves gifts of grace. Many would affirm that our

What would Calvin say to those who say self-motivated decision is a necessary component of salvation?

The Brightness of Human Virtue

"For if the stars, which seem so very bright at night, lose their brilliance in the sight of the sun, what do we think will happen even to the rarest innocence of man when it is compared with God's purity?" (III:XII:4).

Distrust Yourself

"For we will never have enough confidence in him unless we become deeply distrustful of ourselves" (III:XII:8).

What is the relationship between confidence in God and distrust of ourselves?

salvation is a gift of God's grace but that we must decide, we must choose to receive that gift.

SUMMARY XII: GOD'S JUDGMENT SEAT

Against those who might suggest that there is any merit in human goodness, Calvin invited his readers to imagine God's judgment seat, where the value of human works will be seen for what it is. As long as humans compare their behavior with one another, Calvin suggested, they may find some reason for confidence in their own righteousness, but such confidence is shown as an empty illusion in the presence of the utter purity and majesty of God.

Calvin explained that the gravity of God's judgment puts an end to any delusion of the merits of human goodness. Reminding his readers of Jesus' parable of the publican and the Pharisee, Calvin affirmed that the publican's dependence on divine mercy and his acknowledgment of his own sin saved him. Calvin urged his readers to a genuine humility before God that leaves no room for arrogance and complacency about our own righteousness.

COMMENTARY

Calvin's conclusion to this chapter provides another example of his creativity, offering his readers a colorful image that vividly reveals the foolishness and arrogance of those who trust their own merits to justify them before God. Such foolish people, Calvin said, are like a wall congratulating itself for creating the sunbeam that shines through its window. Just as the wall had nothing to do with the origin of the sunbeam, believers have nothing to do with the creation of their own righteousness.

SUMMARY XIII: TWO NOTES ON JUSTIFICATION

Calvin established two focal concerns as a context for all that he wrote about justification: (1) The glory of God is to be preeminent, not diminished in any way by an arrogant attentiveness to the "glory" of human merit. (2) The consciences of believers should have peaceful tranquillity in the presence of God's judgment.

Calvin sought to protect the glory of God by putting no stock at all in the goodness and merits of humans. While affirming the terrifying threat of the judgment of God, Calvin nevertheless assured his readers that their consciences can rest secure by embracing God's promises offered in the gospel.

COMMENTARY

This brief chapter reveals Calvin pastoral motivation for his flock as it seeks to provide them a solid place to rest in the assurance of God's grace. Calvin's concern was that those who suggest that justification is in any way tied to human merit place themselves on an endless, anxious treadmill of works. Since humans can never be "good enough" to merit justification, Calvin insisted that those who mingle human merit with the merit of Christ will never be secure in their salvation.

SUMMARY XIV: NO JUSTIFICATION BY HUMAN RIGHTEOUSNESS

Calvin emphasized the sharpness of God's demands and the gravity of human sin, reminding his readers that no person is able to muster enough righteousness to be justified before God. As a matter of fact, said Calvin, even works

Passive Faith

"For, as regards justification, faith is something merely passive, bringing nothing of ours to the recovering of God's favor but receiving from Christ that which we lack" (III:XIII:5).

What is the foundation of peace with God?

Not Enough

"Men's whole righteousness, gathered together in one heap, could not make compensation for a single sin" (III:XIV:13).

"God, who is rich in mercy, made us alive with Christ even when we were dead in transgressions—it is by grace you have been saved" (Eph. 2:4–5).

A Word to the Professors

"Indeed, it is not very laborious for these leisured rabbis to dispute these matters under the shade in easy chairs. But when that supreme Judge sits in his judgment seat such windy opinions will have to vanish. It is this that we had to seek: what confidence we can bring to his judgment seat in our defense, not what we can talk about in the schools and corners" (III:XIV:15).

of exceptional virtue are reckoned before God's righteousness as sins.

In response to the question, What about the good works of unbelievers? Calvin affirmed that anything good the unregenerate accomplish occurs as a gift of God, the Author of all goodness. Calvin explained that apart from faith no true virtue can possibly exist. And he compared the good works of unbelievers to a runner off course: Despite how much good effort the runner may exert, he continues to run further and further away from his goal.

On the other hand, Calvin did affirm that in the lives of the regenerate works do serve a helpful purpose, strengthening the faith of believers and showing the fruit of regeneration. But he was quick to remind his readers that even the believer's ability to do good is itself a gift of God's grace and therefore no foundation for self-confidence for believers.

 COMMENTARY

Calvin spent twenty pages essentially reaffirming what he had already taught in previous chapters. For Calvin, if believers do not have an accurate understanding of themselves as those who can do nothing to obtain their own salvation, they naturally become arrogant, ungrateful, and deluded into thinking that they are somehow good enough to deserve God's favor.

In this chapter, Calvin took the time to drive home his conviction that apart from the saving work of Christ we are all dead in our sin. And, of course, those who are dead can do absolutely nothing to make themselves alive. For Calvin, the gospel message is not a matter of God's extending His hand to those who are drowning and willing to reach out for help. It is, rather, a matter of God's diving thousands of feet under water to bring to life those who are already dead.

In this chapter, Calvin also revealed the importance of a believer's being rooted in a theology that is more than the mere acceptance of ideas. In his refutation of the ideas of the scholastics, he attacked those who enjoy leisurely, "windy" disputations on theology without the humility of those who know they will one day stand before the terrifying judgment seat of God.

What effect does our contemplating standing before the judgment seat of Christ have on the way we do theology?

SUMMARY XV: THE DANGERS OF A DOCTRINE OF HUMAN MERIT

Leaning on the writings of Augustine and Bernard of Clairvaux, Calvin sought to destroy the common delusion that some form of works for righteousness is included in the doctrine of justification. He reaffirmed that works for righteousness consists of the complete and perfect observance of the Law, a condition no one, other than Christ, has ever achieved. Calvin declared that those who accept even a particle of works for righteousness remove the praise believers owe to God for the freely given gift of justification and remove any firm assurance of salvation for the believer.

COMMENTARY

Calvin's goal throughout the *Institutes* was to help believers gain a solid grounding from which to progress in their faith. Though he spent what may seem to modern readers like an inordinate amount of time proving the believers' utter dependence on God for salvation, he did so

The Sole Foundation

"We experience such participation in him that, although we are still foolish in ourselves, he is our wisdom before God; while we are sinners, he is our righteousness; while we are unclean, he is our purity; while we are weak, . . . yet ours is that power which has been given him in heaven and on earth . . . ; while we still bear about with us the body of death, he is our life. In brief, because all his things are ours and we have all things in him, in us there is nothing" (III:XV:5).

In Calvin's view, what is the "sole foundation" on which we should build our faith?

Not Without Works

"Thus it is clear how true it is that we are justified not without works yet not through works, since in our sharing in Christ which justifies us, sanctification is just as much included as righteousness" (III:XVI:1).

Everything Else Is Rubbish

"What is more, I consider everything a loss compared to the surpassing greatness of knowing Christ Jesus my Lord, for whose sake I have lost all things. I consider them rubbish, that I may gain Christ" (Phil. 3:8).

because he was convinced that this one doctrine is the "sole foundation" on which we should build our faith.

SUMMARY XVI: OBJECTIONS TO THE DOCTRINE OF JUSTIFICATION

Calvin responded to the primary objection to his doctrine of justification, namely that the doctrine of free forgiveness of sins invites people to sin and takes away all motivation for good works. He clarified that the processes of justification and sanctification are joined together by an "indissoluble bond," so believers cannot grasp one without the other.

 COMMENTARY

Calvin did not clearly affirm the importance of good works for the believer until he had, for eight hundred pages, driven home the idea that no one is justified before God by his own works. He ended this chapter by pounding in the point one last time that human works must always be understood as subordinate ("dung") to God's glory and mercy.

SUMMARY XVII: THE PLACE OF WORKS

Calvin explained that when he taught justification by faith alone, he did not abolish the need for good works. Rather, he sought to prevent believers from glorying in their own works or seeking their salvation through them. He recognized "the double acceptance of man before God," seeing in the gospel's promises not only the forgiveness of sins but also the power to make the good works of believers pleasing to God.

Calvin declared that anyone in the Scripture who is said to have pleased God did so only because of God's grace, God's embracing the very works which He Himself had bestowed on believers. Good works are pleasing to God, Calvin insists, only after sin has been pardoned, since justification by faith is the foundation of any righteous works.

In this chapter Calvin responded to the most thorny objection to his doctrine of justification, namely the passage from James that teaches that believers are "justified by works." Calvin explained that although James and Paul use the word *justify* in different ways, their essential messages agree with each other. James, said Calvin, was not speaking of the *way* Christians are justified. Rather, James was rejecting the empty belief of those who show no evidence of their faith. Though good works may be evidence of justification, Calvin cautioned that works must never be confused as being its cause.

COMMENTARY

Again in this chapter Calvin looked to Scripture as the primary foundation for his doctrine. In instances when the Scripture might seem to contradict itself, Calvin sought to find agreement between the various passages so that any apparent contradiction may be removed. He urged his readers to discern in the Bible the sole foundation for their faith and behavior and to approach the Bible with the knowledge that it does not and cannot contradict itself.

In this light, Calvin approached the apparent disagreement between Paul and James by affirming that they cannot be in conflict with each other, since the same Spirit spoke through

How did Calvin answer his critics' charges that his teaching regarding salvation undercuts the motivation for good works?

Our Anchor

"For our assurance, our glory, and the sole anchor of our salvation are that Christ the Son of God is ours" (III:XVII:1).

Justification Defined

"But we define justification as follows: the sinner, received into communion with Christ, is reconciled to God by his grace, while, cleansed by Christ's blood, he obtains forgiveness of sins, and clothed with Christ's righteousness as if it were his own, he stands confident before the heavenly judgment seat. After forgiveness of sins is set forth, the good works that now follow are appraised otherwise than on their own merit" (III:XVII:8).

How did Calvin see the apparent conflict between James and Paul regarding justification by works?

The Agreement of Scripture

"Here I beseech the godly, if they know the true rule of righteousness is to be sought from the Scripture alone, religiously and earnestly to ponder with me how Scripture may, without quibbling, be duly brought into agreement with itself" (III:XVII:8).

By Faith Alone

"By faith alone not only we ourselves but our works as well are justified" (III:XVII:10).

What principle of biblical interpretation did Calvin rest on in dealing with apparent disagreements on how humans are made right with God?

both of them. For Calvin, it was impossible that Christ speaking through Paul and Christ speaking through James could disagree.

Perhaps surprisingly, Calvin did, in this chapter, provide a place for the righteousness of works. Once justification by faith is firmly established and good works are no longer appraised on their own merit, Calvin freely admitted that the life of obedience is an essential (though not causal) component of the Christian life.

SUMMARY XVIII: WORKS RIGHTEOUSNESS AND REWARD

Calvin explained that God's many promises to reward obedience do not in any way make works the cause of salvation, since God's mercy came before the works. Believers, said Calvin, do not receive rewards as wages for their works but as an inheritance promised to those who have been adopted as sons and daughters. Calvin affirmed that believers are like the workers in Christ's parable of the vineyard, not being paid based on the merits of their own labor but out of the riches of the master's goodness.

Calvin affirmed that reward is promised to encourage and comfort believers, reminding them that God is a "faithful custodian" who will repay, with "plentiful interest," all they have invested with Him. To awake our sluggishness, Calvin explained, God has given the assurance that, whatever affliction believers endure, their suffering is not in vain and will not be lacking a reward in heaven.

COMMENTARY

Calvin's main purpose in this chapter was to fortify his readers' confidence in God and in the assurance of God's abundant rewards. But he was careful not to suggest that God is our debtor, that He somehow rewards believers because they deserve it or because their works merit His reward. Consistent with his overall doctrine of justification, Calvin sought to remove in believers any empty confidence in themselves that they might cast themselves fully on the free mercy of God.

SUMMARY XIX: CHRISTIAN FREEDOM

Calvin identified three forms of Christian freedom:

1. Freedom from the Law—Since Christian justification is not about how we become righteous but how we will be reckoned righteous before God, we are therefore free from the Law's demands of perfect obedience to trust in God's mercy alone.

2. Freedom to obey the Law—Because we have been adopted as sons, we are invited by our Father to offer our joyful obedience, even though such obedience will always be incomplete and imperfect.

3. Freedom to be indifferent about indifferent things—As regards matters not specifically commended to us in the Bible, we are free from superstitious worry and confusion, free to use them or not to use them, indifferently.

Calvin balanced his emphasis on Christian freedom with a warning that this freedom must not be used as a license for luxury or gluttony, though he refrained from a blanket

God's Rewards

"God 'will give to each person according to what he has done'" (Rom. 2:6).

"Our works are pleasing only through pardon" (III:XVIII:5).

Does Faith Justify?

"We say that faith justifies, not because it merits righteousness for us by its own worth, but because it is an instrument whereby we obtain free the righteousness of Christ" (III:XVIII:8).

If works don't make a person right with God, does God reward good works?

condemnation of the wealthy over the poor. He insisted that even in regard to indifferent things we are to limit our freedom if it becomes a cause of injury to our neighbors or a cause of stumbling for weaker Christians. Calvin also condemns any attempt to use Christian freedom as a license to make us less subject to human laws or civil government.

Freedom's Priority

"But freedom is especially an appendage of justification and is of no little avail in understanding its power. Indeed, those who seriously fear God will enjoy the incomparable benefit of this doctrine. . . . Unless this freedom be comprehended, neither Christ nor gospel truth, no inner peace of soul, can be rightly known" (III:XIX:1).

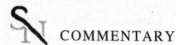

COMMENTARY

Calvin ended his doctrine of justification with his reflections on Christian freedom, affirming that godly freedom is the proper result of our justification. These reflections seem far from a caricature of Calvin as a pessimistic, rigid, and even legalistic theologian. Consistent with his central message throughout the *Institutes*, here again he emphasized the good news that brings comfort, certain assurance, and true freedom.

By positioning his reflections on Christian freedom at the end of his major section on justification, he resisted his readers' becoming mired in self-centered groveling and pushed them forward toward a joyous obedience before God. Despite the fact that many may abuse Christian freedom and use it as a license for unbridled disobedience, Calvin resisted the temptation to minimize the importance of this doctrine.

What three forms of Christian freedom did Calvin identify?

Calvin's unique emphasis on "the freedom to be indifferent about indifferent things" provides the kind of focused language that has had the power to raise a banner to call Christians of various perspectives to find the central core of orthodox Christianity. As a basis for determining which things are essential and what are "indifferent," Calvin followed the pattern he had established throughout his work, consistently sending his readers back to the Scripture.

ORIGINAL LATIN EDITIONS
Christianae Relgionis Institutio (Basel: Platter and Lasius, 1536).

Institutio Christianae Religionis (Strasbourg: Rihel, 1539, 1543).

Institutio Totius Christianae Religionis (Geneva: Girard, 1550).

Institutio Christianae Religionis (Geneva: Estienne, 1559).

ORIGINAL FRENCH EDITIONS
Institution de la Religion Chrestienne (Geneva: Girard, 1541, 1545).

Institution de la Religion Chrestienne (Geneva: Crespin, 1560).

ENGLISH TRANSLATIONS
Thomas Norton, trans., *The Institution of Christian Religion* (London: Wolfe and Harrison, 1561, and multiple editions to 1762).

John Allen, trans., *Institutes of the Christian Religion* (London: Walker, 1813 with multiple editions in America up to Philadelphia: Westminster Press, 1936).

Henry Beveridge, *The Institutes of the Christian Religion* (Edinburgh: Calvin Translation Society, 1845; with reprints in America by Grand Rapids: Wm. B. Eerdmans Publishing Company).

F. W. Battles and J. T. McNeill (trans. and ed.), *Calvin: Institutes of the Christian Religion*, 2 vols. (The Library of Christian Classics, vols. XX–XXI, Philadelphia, 1960).

COMMENTARIES
E. A. Dowey, *The Knowledge of God in Calvin's Theology* (New York, 1952).

B. B. Warfield, *Calvin and Calvinism* (New York, 1931).

F. Wendel, Calvin: *The Origin and Development of His Religious Thought* (New York, 1963).

BIOGRAPHY

Timothy George, *Theology of the Reformers* (Nashville: Broadman Press, 1988).

Alister E. McGrath, *A Life of John Calvin* (Baker Book House, 1990).

T. H. L. Parker, *John Calvin* (J. M. Dent & Sons, 1975).

SHEPHERD'S NOTES